Advance pr.
The Sustainability Chan

Bob Willard has written a stunning co...pnation of experience-based wisdom: his and that of other leaders who have done real things to work towards organizational change and sustainability in business. *The Sustainability Champion's Guidebook* is spot on for all levels of an organization, from high-level vision right down to individual, personal behavior. Read this book to jump-start or speed your journey to a better future.

— Ray Anderson, Founder and Chairman, Interface Inc.,
and author of *Mid-Course Correction*

"Sustainability" is *what* needs to be changed but then there is the matter of *how* to go about implementing such a dramatic shift so that its benefits are fully realized. This book goes beyond explaining the basics of sustainability; it outlines key issues that surface when navigating the human landscape of such an endeavor.

— Daryl Conner, Chairman, Conner Partners, and author of
Managing at the Speed of Change and *Leading at the Edge of Chaos*

Like all good writers, Bob Willard has put into words what we know but haven't been able to articulate: Sustainability has moved beyond changing the mindset of management to become a mainstream driver of innovation and competitive advantage *if* you have the know-how to act on it. By applying the wisdom of this book, readers will find new ways to create sustainable value. A must-read during times of economic crisis.

— Chris Laszlo, Managing Partner, Sustainable Value Partners,
and author of *The Sustainable Company* and *Sustainable Value*

If you are working to implement sustainability in your organization then you simply must read this book. It provides clear guidance and simple, yet powerful, advice for getting the job done. Bob writes with wisdom based on experience.

— Andrew W. Savitz, author of *The Triple Bottom Line*

To step up to leadership requires primarily competence rather than a change of values. Bob Willard doesn't turn to those who still haven't got it but to those who need to know just how — from envisioning to structuring, through elegant transition processes. It's the best out there.

— Karl-Henrik Robèrt, Founder of The Natural Step
and author of *The Natural Step Story*

A compelling read for those who are just starting their sustainability journey up Mount Sustainability, graphically pointing out the likely encounters that you will experience along the way. And for those like myself who started their journey with just the bare essentials of The Natural Step Framework, this book brings to life all those subliminal thoughts that make you think that Bob was right behind you the whole time.

— Dr Jason Leadbitter, Sustainability Manager, Ineos ChlorVinyls

Bob Willard provides a roadmap for effective leadership that is both authoritative and accessible. Corporate sustainability evolution just clicked into overdrive.

— Joel Makower, Executive Editor, GreenBiz.com,
and author of *Strategies for the Green Economy*

Happily, mainstream business education schools are finally embracing sustainable development. Bob Willard's new book is the perfect companion text of leadership tips and techniques for business leaders aspiring to lead the next industrial revolution. It should be a compulsory text in all business schools.

— Hunter Lovins, Founder and President, Natural Capitalism, Inc.,
and co-author of *Natural Capitalism* and *Factor Four*

After inspiring us with his first two books on the "why" of corporate sustainability, Bob Willard has completed the trilogy with an excellent book on the "how." Full of practical and proven advice for leading the transformation from within organizations, this book can transform you too — into a successful champion. Read it; absorb it; do it!

— Brian Kelly, Director, Sustainable Enterprise Academy,
Schulich School of Business, York University

All over the world, Boards of Directors are starting to take account of sustainability issues as never before. The question now is "how?" not "why?" Hence the need for this guidebook — from one of the most experienced sustainability practitioners on the block.

> — Jonathon Porritt, Founder Director, Forum for the Future,
> and Chairman, UK Sustainable Development Commission

Concise, comprehensive, and compelling, this book distills a tremendous amount of theoretical and practical information into a well-chiseled guide that is exceedingly useful — and wise.

> — Alan AtKisson, author of *Believing Cassandra*
> and *The ISIS Agreement*

Bob Willard is a champion guide. Learn how to keep your organization on today's rails, but also help lay new ones — exploring future pathways to real value and wealth.

> — John Elkington, Co-Founder of ENDS, SustainAbility, and Volans,
> and author of *The Power of Unreasonable People*
> and *The Phoenix Economy*

Creating sustainable organizations is one of the most urgent and important missions of our time. Bob Willard embraces the challenge with passion, energy, and determination. This is not a book you should just buy. It's a book you must use. Now. We don't have time to wait.

> — Jim Kouzes, Dean's Executive Professor of Leadership,
> Leavey School of Business, Santa Clara University,
> and co-author of *The Leadership Challenge*

The sustainability revolution will be led by committed champions who achieve impact beyond their titles and formal roles. Here you will find the hands-on practices, processes, and techniques needed to drive the transformation to sustainability in your organization.

> — Stuart L. Hart, S.C. Johnson Chair
> in Sustainable Global Enterprise,
> the Johnson School, Cornell University,
> and author of *Capitalism at the Crossroads*

Sustainability professionals have long understood that helping organizations become more sustainable is a formidable change-management challenge. Bob Willard is a catalyst for this type of change, and in this book he uses his methodical, frank, and engaging style to provide the reader with considerable insight and practical advice on how we too can become champions for change.

— Kevin Brady, Director,
Five Winds International

Once again, Bob Willard has provided much-needed, timely insights and advice on how a business can move toward sustainability. This book hits the bull's-eye.

— Bob Doppelt, Director, Resource Innovations and
The Climate Leadership Initiative, Institute for a
Sustainable Environment, University of Oregon,
and author of *Leading Change toward Sustainability*

Willard's book is a valuable guide for anyone seeking to integrate principles of sustainability into their organizational culture. It is practical, straightforward, and insightful. This book is an easy way to access some proven practices for creating sustainable organizations.

— Brian and Mary Nattrass, authors of *The Natural Step
for Business* and *Dancing with the Tiger*

Bob Willard has summarized years of experience, insight, and knowledge into a useful tool for those of us struggling to transform sustainability ideas into reality within complex organizations. This is a must read.

— Barb Steele, Director,
Canadian Business for Social Responsibility

Just as his previous books have provided the analytical tools to help readers build sustainability into financial management. Bob Willard's new book brings comparable clarity and practicality to the even more difficult and essential challenge of building sustainability into corporate culture.

— Gil Friend, President and CEO, Natural Logic Inc.,
and author of *The Truth About Green Business*

THE
SUSTAINABILITY
CHAMPION'S
GUIDEBOOK

HOW TO TRANSFORM YOUR COMPANY

BOB WILLARD

Todd,

Best wishes!

Bob Willard

08/10/09

NEW SOCIETY PUBLISHERS

Cataloging in Publication Data

A catalog record for this publication is available
from the National Library of Canada.

Cover design by Diane McIntosh
Cover images: leaf – © iStock/Wojtek Kryczka;
target – © istock/Hector Daniel Stilman

Printed in Canada by Friesens.
First printing May 2009.

New Society Publishers acknowledges the support of the Government of Canada
through the Book Publishing Industry Development Program (BPIDP)
for our publishing activities.

Paperback ISBN: 978-0-86571-658-2

Inquiries regarding requests
to reprint all or part of *The Sustainability Champion's Guidebook*
should be addressed to New Society Publishers at the address below.

To order directly from the publishers,
please call toll-free (North America) 1-800-567-6772,
or order online at www.newsociety.com

Any other inquiries can be directed by mail to:
New Society Publishers
P.O. Box 189, Gabriola Island, BC V0R 1X0, Canada
(250) 247-9737

New Society Publishers' mission is to publish books that contribute in fundamental
ways to building an ecologically sustainable and just society, and to do so with the
least possible impact on the environment, in a manner that models this vision. We are
committed to doing this not just through education, but through action. This book
is one step toward ending global deforestation and climate change. It is printed on
Forest Stewardship Council-certified acid-free paper that is **100% post-consumer
recycled** (100% old growth forest-free), processed chlorine free, and printed with
vegetable-based, low-VOC inks, with covers produced using FSC-certified stock.
Additionally, New Society purchases carbon offsets based on an annual audit,
operating with a carbon-neutral footprint. For further information, or to browse our
full list of books and purchase securely, visit our website at: www.newsociety.com

NEW SOCIETY PUBLISHERS
www.newsociety.com

Mixed Sources
Cert no. SW-COC-001271
© 1996 FSC
FSC

DEDICATION

To the memory of Bill Alexander,
whose gentle influence
opened up life-changing possibilities for me.

Contents

Foreword

We are entering an era of new hopes and new fears. Both demand strategic but well-grounded action. This action may come initially from deep concern, fear, or even a sense of panic. But to be sustainable over time, our actions must ultimately be connected to our positive aspirations — perhaps, for example, our choice to ensure that people, communities, and all of nature can flourish indefinitely. Our choices, when aligned with those things that are most important to us, allow us to invest our life spirit and energy in our actions, and to do so with effectiveness, clarity, and a sense of purpose.

There has been much debate about whether we can move directly to behaviorial change and action, or whether we must first change our attitudes and beliefs. With regard to sustainability, that debate is over. Anyone who cares about the future and is also aware of the current state of our local and global systems knows it is time to exercise personal leadership, learn new behaviors, and get moving. Bob Willard's advice and direct guidance in this book reveal a suite of actions you can take to connect your vision and commitment to the real world.

The profound change we see is unfolding around different kinds of meeting tables. Many executives report that the kitchen table at home, where their kids are now regularly challenging them to accelerate the actions they take at work to advance sustainability, is as demanding as the boardroom table at work, where company directors push hard for fundamental change and rethinking at every level. There are also thousands of meeting-room tables in organizations around the world where front-line employees, supervisors, and middle managers gather regularly. You can put Bob Willard's tools directly to work at any of these tables. In fact, his guidance can be seen as table stakes for making progress and accelerating action.

Bob's suggestions help you bring a sense of urgency to all these discussions. One of the key attributes of climate change is that it is clearly measurable. We can see that the atmospheric "bathtub" of greenhouse gases is filling up far too fast and will soon overflow if we don't engage mainstream corporate resources and influence to help us turn off the taps of emissions. The same is true in the other "big three" arenas of sustainability — food and water, materials and waste, and social equity. That's why Bob cuts to the chase in this book. He provides specific directions, checklists, and tips to get on with the work, based on his depth of experience in seeing what is needed.

At the foundation of Bob Willard's work is his recognition of the need to engage employees at all levels. The magic behind organizational culture change is employee buy-in. The essence of the leadership practices and paradoxes in this book is employee engagement. That principle is true whether you are leading the change from the middle, the bottom, or the top of the corporate hierarchy. By definition, without widespread engagement throughout the company, there is no culture change. Grasping that fundamental truth will enable sustainability champions to accelerate the necessary transformation/revolution.

Bob understands how to apply leadership practices to corporate transformation. He knows how effective leadership works. This book applies the wisdom of hundreds of leadership experts to the specific challenge of leading the transformation to become a sustainable enterprise. A sustainable enterprise is a learning organization in the most profound sense. It embraces approaches that foster the five disciplines of a learning organization and unleashes the creative potential of the workforce. This unleashing provides the basis for what could be called grounded hope — hope that is nourished by the satisfaction of tangible actions, progress, and results on the front lines of sustainability; hope that is directly connected to personal and collective leadership and action to produce a flourishing, sustainable world. My sincere thanks to Bob for giving us all the gift of grounded hope.

— Bryan Smith

Co-author of *The Necessary Revolution*,
The Dance of Change, and *The Fifth Discipline Fieldbook*.

Acknowledgments

This guidebook synthesizes my leadership experience at IBM with my more recent experience engaging organizations in sustainability transformations.

During my 34-year career at IBM Canada, I had the opportunity to participate in changes of various magnitudes in a large, established company. My last ten years at IBM were in its Leadership Development department, training managers and executives to be more effective business leaders and change agents. In that role, I summarized the best books on personal and organizational leadership and integrated their guidance into IBM's leadership development training. I owe a significant debt of gratitude to my many IBM colleagues for the opportunity to learn with them about effectively leading organizational change.

Since I took early retirement in 2000, my formal studies, writing, and speaking have been about the business case for sustainability. I have given hundreds of talks at conferences, where I have had the privilege to learn from sustainability experts. Plus, I continue to read extensively about leading organizational change to a culture of sustainability. I thank the sustainability speakers and authors, especially those cited throughout this book, for their insights.

I serve on the core faculty of the Sustainable Enterprise Academy sponsored by York University's Schulich School of Business. Countless discussions with colleagues and corporate attendees reinforced my sense that companies could transform to sustainable enterprises using organizational change approaches.

Finally, my son, Graham, contributed greatly to the readability and quality of the manuscript with his insightful edits and candid feedback. Thank you all.

CHAPTER 1

The Sustainability Challenge Is a Leadership Challenge

- The Urgent Need for a Practical Guidebook

- Leadership Practices for Sustainability Champions

- An Unsustainable Company

- A Sustainable Company

- Transforming from a Stage 3 Company to a Stage 4 Company

- The Big Four Sustainability Challenges

- Culture Change Framework

1

I am concerned that we are running out of time. Leading economists who study the economics of climate change, people like Nicholas Stern, say that we have 10 to 20 years before we reach an irreversible tipping point (Figure 1.0). Parts of the world are losing access to food and water and experiencing other severe resource, climate, population, and health problems. In isolation, each crisis is not good; combined, they are a troubling mix. Rather than improving, things seem to be worsening. So, in short, we need to crank up the urgency, stop the talking and hand-wringing, and get on with making our world more sustainable. As the most influential actors on the planet, companies must lead by example by adopting sustainable economic, environmental, and social practices. Quickly.

A few companies (3 to 5 percent) are already taking the lead. However, we need more enterprises to join the movement so that we have a critical mass (20 percent) of enlightened enterprises on board. We will only achieve unstoppable momentum if sustainability champions become more effective leaders.

Sustainability champions/leaders are looking for help, and they are understandably impatient. They seek a prescriptive distillation of lessons learned from others — an abridged field guide of tips for transforming organizational culture from unsustainability to sustainability, without all the supporting anecdotes and case studies. That is what this guidebook provides.

Despite the urgent need for corporate transformations, the change leadership style advocated throughout this book is decentralized and non-directive. It is courageously soft. That is why it works and enables companies to rapidly develop winning sustainability strategies, breakthrough products, and innovative services.

FIGURE 1.0

Stern Review: The Climate Change Situation Is Urgent

There is still time to avoid the worst impacts of climate change, if we take strong action now. The scientific evidence is now overwhelming: climate change is a serious global threat, and it *demands an urgent global response.*

The evidence gathered by the [Stern Review report] leads to a simple conclusion: *the benefits of strong and early action far outweigh the economic costs of not acting.* Climate change will affect the basic elements of life for people around the world — access to water, food production, health, and the environment....

If we don't act, the overall costs and risks of climate change will be equivalent to losing at least 5% of global GDP each year, now and forever. If a wider range of risks and impacts is taken into account, the estimates of damage could rise to 20% of GDP or more.

In contrast, the costs of action — reducing greenhouse gas emissions to avoid the worst impacts of climate change — can be limited to around 1% of global GDP each year. The investment that takes place in the *next 10–20 years* will have a profound effect on the climate in the second half of this century and in the next. *Our actions now and over the coming decades could create risks of major disruption to economic and social activity, on a scale similar to those associated with the great wars and the economic depression of the first half of the 20th century. And it will be difficult or impossible to reverse these changes. So prompt and strong action is clearly warranted.*

Source: Nicholas Stern, *The Economics of Climate Change,* Cambridge University Press, 2006, pp. vi–ix (italics added).

Sustainability champions are found throughout corporate hierarchies. They have a passion about sustainability and they aspire to persuade their companies to become model sustainable enterprises. They want their companies to be a more positive force in the world. Often they hold junior or middle management positions in their organizations and lack the authority to effect the necessary changes. Understanding that leadership is a role, not a position, they cleverly exert their influence and convince the right people to help make it happen.

Sustainability champions promote the dialogue that creates the culture change and governance transformations necessary for a company to be truly sustainable. They are change makers. They use strategies and tactics from the arsenal of effective organizational development practitioners, social marketers, team builders, and learning organization leaders. They transform their companies into more sustainable corporate citizens with better products, more responsible services, and more inclusive governance approaches.

Another appropriate label for these leaders is "sustainability intrapreneurs." Intrapreneurs apply entrepreneurial approaches within existing large organizations.[1] Sustainability intrapreneurs integrate environmental and social values and behaviors deeply into their companies. I will use the labels "sustainability champion" and "sustainability intrapreneur" interchangeably.

The sustainability challenge is a leadership challenge. Sustainability champions/intrapreneurs apply The Five Practices of Exemplary Leadership®, outlined in Figure 1.1, to sustainability challenges in their organizations. This guidebook elaborates on how to do that, echoing the five leadership practices in its suggested steps, practices, paradoxes, and advice on how to avoid derailers.

FIGURE 1.1

Kouzes and Posner: The Five Practices of Exemplary Leadership®

1. **Model the Way**
   - Clarify values by finding your voice and affirming shared ideals.
   - Set the example by aligning actions with shared values.

2. **Inspire a Shared Vision**
   - Envision the future by imagining exciting and ennobling possibilities.
   - Enlist others in a common vision by appealing to shared aspirations.

3. **Challenge the Process**
   - Search for opportunities by seizing the initiative and by looking outward for innovative ways to improve.
   - Experiment and take risks by constantly generating small wins and learning from experience.

4. **Enable Others to Act**
   - Foster collaboration by building trust and facilitating relationships.
   - Strengthen others by increasing self-determination and developing competence.

5. **Encourage the Heart**
   - Recognize contributions by showing appreciation for individual excellence.
   - Celebrate the values and victories by creating a spirit of community.

Source: James M. Kouzes and Barry Z. Posner, *The Leadership Challenge*, Jossey-Bass, p. 26. Copyright © 2007. Reproduced by permission of John Wiley and Sons, Inc. The Five Practices of Exemplary Leadership® is a registered trademark of James M. Kouzes and Barry Z. Posner.

How would you know an unsustainable enterprise if you saw one? Unfortunately, it would look like today's take-make-waste norm, as portrayed in Figure 1.2. That model is not working. That is, it violates all four of the Natural Step's systems conditions for a sustainable society.[2]

1. It contributes directly or indirectly to the systematic increase in the concentrations of *waste from substances extracted from the earth's crust*, such as heavy metals, fossil fuels, and byproducts from their use.

2. It contributes directly or indirectly to systematic increases in concentrations of hazardous and non-hazardous *waste from substances produced by society*, such as over 70,000 chemicals, dioxins, and PCBs.

3. It contributes directly or indirectly to systematic *overextraction and degradation of nature by physical means*, such as deforestation, over-harvesting of fisheries, and depletion of farm lands.

4. It contributes directly or indirectly to abuses of political or economic power in society so that *human needs are not met* for such things as clean air, potable water, nutritious food, adequate shelter, and quality of life.

The indirect contributions referenced above occur in the company's supply chain and its distribution system to end users. They include the company's ecological footprint from its indirect consumption of water, energy, and raw materials throughout its value chain. Corporate accountability for supply chain impacts is a recent sustainability demand from important stakeholders.

Unsustainable capitalism is a fun game for some, but it causes too much collateral damage in the environmental and social spheres. We need a more responsible game plan.

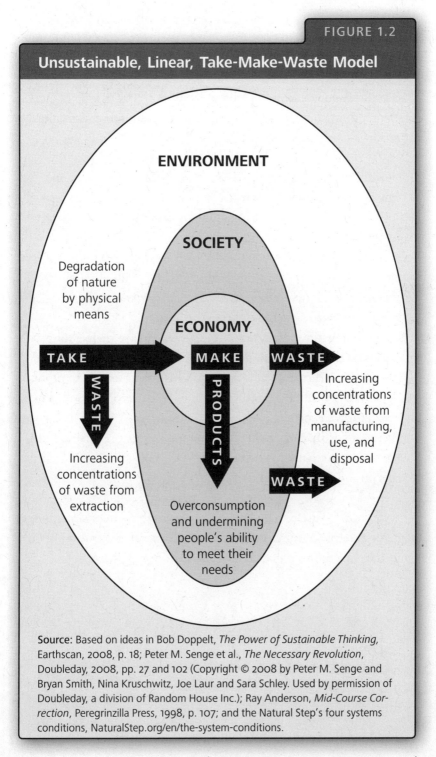

FIGURE 1.2

Unsustainable, Linear, Take-Make-Waste Model

ENVIRONMENT

SOCIETY

Degradation of nature by physical means

ECONOMY

TAKE → MAKE WASTE →

WASTE ↓

PRODUCTS ↓

Increasing concentrations of waste from extraction

WASTE →

Increasing concentrations of waste from manufacturing, use, and disposal

Overconsumption and undermining people's ability to meet their needs

Source: Based on ideas in Bob Doppelt, *The Power of Sustainable Thinking*, Earthscan, 2008, p. 18; Peter M. Senge et al., *The Necessary Revolution*, Doubleday, 2008, pp. 27 and 102 (Copyright © 2008 by Peter M. Senge and Bryan Smith, Nina Kruschwitz, Joe Laur and Sara Schley. Used by permission of Doubleday, a division of Random House Inc.); Ray Anderson, *Mid-Course Correction*, Peregrinzilla Press, 1998, p. 107; and the Natural Step's four systems conditions, NaturalStep.org/en/the-system-conditions.

A sustainable corporate model differs significantly from today's model. Figure 1.3 shows how it honors Natural Capitalism's four strategies for an authentically sustainable society.[3]

1. **Radical resource productivity:** Companies stretch natural resources by increasing productivity for a given amount of a resource by factors of 5, 10, or 100. This addresses issues of overharvesting and depletion.
2. **Ecological redesign:** Companies use closed-loop production systems so that any waste from production and end-of-life disposal is treated as a resource and reused. Companies acknowledge they can't throw things away because there is no "away."
3. **Service and flow economy:** Companies replace their goods with services. They lease products and their solutions instead of selling them. When the product becomes obsolete or is unable to produce its service, the company takes it back and recycles or remanufactures the returned product.
4. **Investment in natural capital:** Companies restore, maintain, and expand ecosystems to sustain society's needs and avoid social upheaval and costly regulations.

The new borrow-use-return business model is more responsible.[4] A sustainable enterprise aspires to a sustainable corporate blueprint not only in its own operations but also throughout its supply chain.

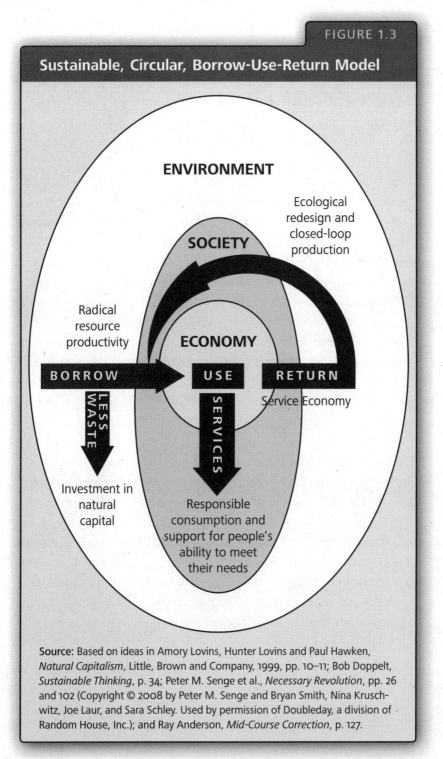

FIGURE 1.3

Sustainable, Circular, Borrow-Use-Return Model

ENVIRONMENT

Ecological redesign and closed-loop production

SOCIETY

Radical resource productivity

ECONOMY

BORROW → USE RETURN

LESS WASTE

SERVICES

Service Economy

Investment in natural capital

Responsible consumption and support for people's ability to meet their needs

Source: Based on ideas in Amory Lovins, Hunter Lovins and Paul Hawken, *Natural Capitalism*, Little, Brown and Company, 1999, pp. 10–11; Bob Doppelt, *Sustainable Thinking*, p. 34; Peter M. Senge et al., *Necessary Revolution*, pp. 26 and 102 (Copyright © 2008 by Peter M. Senge and Bryan Smith, Nina Kruschwitz, Joe Laur, and Sara Schley. Used by permission of Doubleday, a division of Random House, Inc.); and Ray Anderson, *Mid-Course Correction*, p. 127.

Figure 1.4 depicts the sustainability journey for large, publicly traded companies. Corporate sustainability champions usually focus on leading their companies through the intermediate steps between Stages 3 and 4.

- **Stage 3.0:** Improve working conditions and capture eco-efficiencies within the company's internal operations and processes, especially energy efficiencies and carbon footprint reductions.
- **Stage 3.1:** Work with suppliers to improve working conditions and capture eco-efficiencies within suppliers' operations and processes.
- **Stage 3.2:** Work with stakeholders to create innovative sustainable products and services that creatively replace today's unsustainable ones and strategically position the company to capture new markets.
- **Stage 3.3:** Revamp the company's governance system to ensure it aligns with sustainability principles.
- **Stage 4:** Rebrand the company as a sustainable enterprise, with sustainability deeply integrated into its business strategies and culture.

This guidebook shows how to progress through those stages in a way that works for the company's executives, employees, and important stakeholders. The change process transforms "resource-depleting, pollution-spewing," unsustainable companies that are "pushing nature ever closer to collapse — and generating a gaping divide between rich and poor that increasingly defies all conceptions of fairness."[5] Instead, these companies adopt an exciting, sustainable, winning, circular, cradle-to-cradle model of commerce. Sustainability marries philanthropic and ecological motivations with concern for the bottom line. It is smart business.

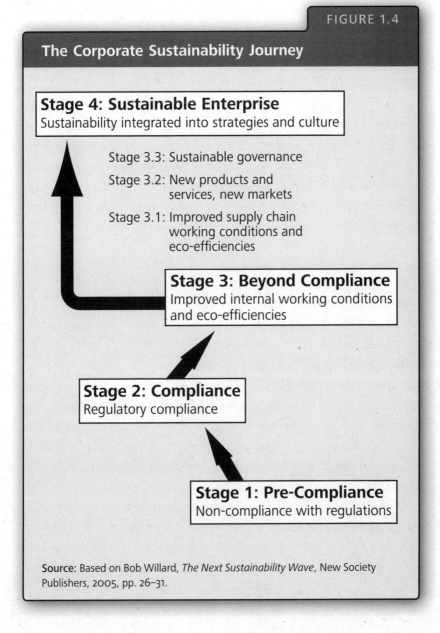

FIGURE 1.4

The Corporate Sustainability Journey

Stage 4: Sustainable Enterprise
Sustainability integrated into strategies and culture

Stage 3.3: Sustainable governance

Stage 3.2: New products and
services, new markets

Stage 3.1: Improved supply chain
working conditions and
eco-efficiencies

Stage 3: Beyond Compliance
Improved internal working conditions
and eco-efficiencies

Stage 2: Compliance
Regulatory compliance

Stage 1: Pre-Compliance
Non-compliance with regulations

Source: Based on Bob Willard, *The Next Sustainability Wave*, New Society
Publishers, 2005, pp. 26–31.

Sustainability is huge, complex, and inclusive. Numerous economic, social, and environmental issues urgently require attention, both within the company and throughout its supply chain. The challenge can be daunting for sustainability champions as they prepare to transform their companies from the unsustainable model in Figure 1.2 to the sustainable model in Figure 1.3. To get the most from their efforts, they need to focus their attention on a few high-leverage areas, the Big Four Sustainability Challenges illustrated in Figure 1.5.[6]

- Energy and Climate Change
- Food and Water
- Waste and Toxicity
- Poverty and Social Justice

Different colleagues and executives will be energized by different sustainability challenges. Go with their instincts. Let them use the challenge they feel is most relevant as a lens on high-leverage areas that provide the biggest payback. For example, if they choose Energy and Climate Change as their sustainability lens, they might set a goal of using breakthrough technologies to become a net supplier of energy back to the grid.

The Big Four Sustainability Challenges let sustainability champions apply the 80–20 rule to their efforts: if they address those issues throughout their value chain, their company will be 80 percent of the way to a culture of sustainability. That is a good start. The last 20 percent of the transformation will quickly follow.

FIGURE 1.5

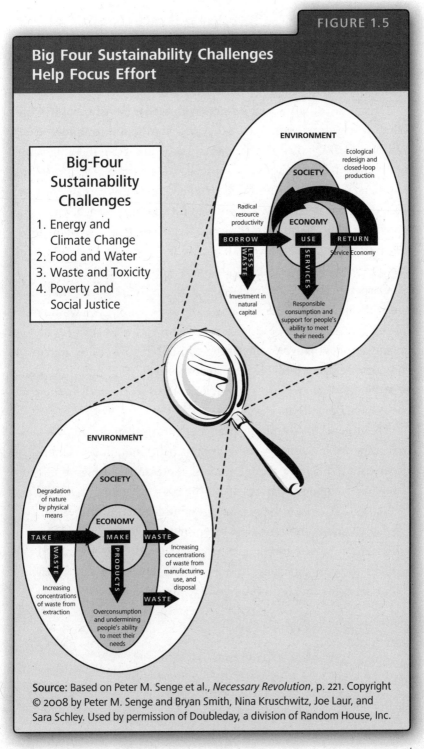

Big Four Sustainability Challenges Help Focus Effort

Big-Four Sustainability Challenges

1. Energy and Climate Change
2. Food and Water
3. Waste and Toxicity
4. Poverty and Social Justice

ENVIRONMENT

SOCIETY

Ecological redesign and closed-loop production

Radical resource productivity

ECONOMY

BORROW → USE RETURN

Service Economy

LESS WASTE

SERVICES

Investment in natural capital

Responsible consumption and support for people's ability to meet their needs

ENVIRONMENT

SOCIETY

ECONOMY

Degradation of nature by physical means

TAKE → MAKE WASTE

WASTE

PRODUCTS

Increasing concentrations of waste from manufacturing, use, and disposal

Increasing concentrations of waste from extraction

WASTE

Overconsumption and undermining people's ability to meet their needs

Source: Based on Peter M. Senge et al., *Necessary Revolution*, p. 221. Copyright © 2008 by Peter M. Senge and Bryan Smith, Nina Kruschwitz, Joe Laur, and Sara Schley. Used by permission of Doubleday, a division of Random House, Inc.

Culture Change Framework

Why are we talking about a "transformation"?

Organizations are social systems with well-established norms and values that govern employees' behaviors. Worthy improvement strategies like Total Quality Management (TQM) and reengineering sometimes failed because they were rejected like a virus by the underlying mindsets, worldviews, and value systems of executives, managers, and staff. Unless sustainability is supported by a culture change, it will end up as another well-intentioned voyage dashed on the rocks of organizational status quo. That is why we have to mess with organizational culture to accomplish a lasting sustainability transformation.

Corporate culture and executives' worldviews are closely linked. Executives will resist culture change for the same reasons you would resist having your worldview changed: it has worked for you until now, and change implies that you were wrong. Most of us are not prepared to admit our mistakes, especially if we are executives. We should not be surprised if skeptical executives do not welcome our offer to help them see the sustainability light.

The urgency of the sustainability situation requires that we clean up irresponsible, unsustainable corporate behavior quickly. Happily, the experience of effective change leaders (represented in Figure 1.6) suggests that changing behaviors first is the most expedient way to change the status quo culture before tackling entrenched norms, values, and fundamental assumptions. The seven-step change process, leadership practices, paradoxes, and derailers that are described in the rest of this guidebook focus on transforming unsustainable corporate behaviors. Cultural norms and assumptions will naturally follow suit.

FIGURE 1.6

Behavioral Approach to Cultural Transformation

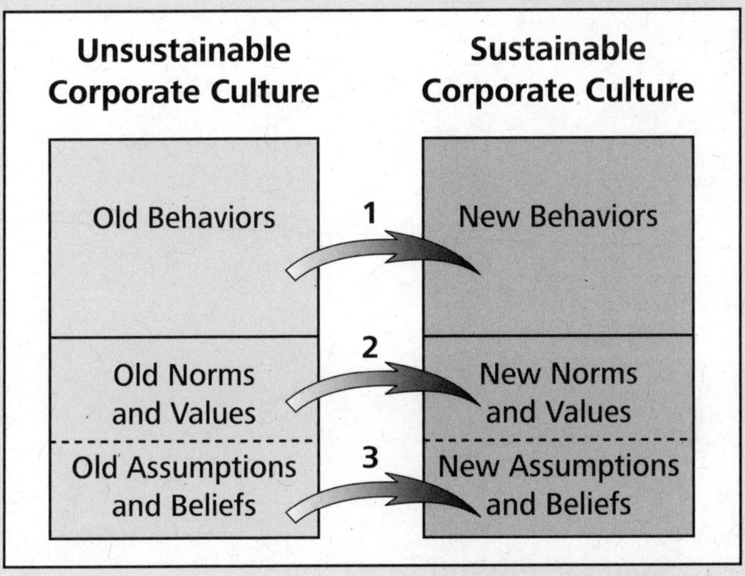

Unsustainable Corporate Culture		Sustainable Corporate Culture
Old Behaviors	**1** →	New Behaviors
Old Norms and Values	**2** →	New Norms and Values
Old Assumptions and Beliefs	**3** →	New Assumptions and Beliefs

Source: Edgar H. Schein, *Organizational Culture and Leadership*, Jossey-Bass, 1985, p. 14.

CHAPTER 2

The Seven-Step Change Process

- Introduction

- Step 1: Wake Up and Decide

- Step 2: Inspire Shared Vision(s)

- Step 3: Assess Current Realities

- Step 4: Develop Strategies

- Step 5: Build the Case(s) for Change

- Step 6: Mobilize Commitment

- Step 7: Embed and Align

The seven steps in Figure 2.0 map the essence of the sustainability change process in any organization. The seven-step process is a scalable meme — it will work for teams, networks, departments, organizations, communities, and societies. That is, you can scale the process to fit organizations of any size that wish to align their behaviors, norms, values, and mindsets with sustainability principles.

Step 1 is personal. You wake up, decide to lead the change, and start to develop expertise that enhances your credibility. Next, you engage an internal network of kindred spirits and refine the visions and cases for change with their help and insights (Steps 2, 3, 4, and 5). Steps 2 through 5 are cyclical, as the arrows in Figure 2.0 suggest. You will repeat them with your network of networks as you progress through the intermediate steps between Stages 3 and 4 of the corporate sustainability journey, as described in Chapter 1.

Then you influence the influencers, who will engage senior management in a similar dialogue with the goal of establishing a powerful, cross-functional Sustainability Team to make the necessary transformation happen (Step 6). In Steps 6 and 7 the hard work of building pervasive support for the change and cementing the new sustainability culture into the company takes place. These steps require the most time because they involve changing mindsets.

Change can be messy, and you will revisit many steps as the journey progresses. Use the steps as navigational aids rather than as a one-directional plan of action. Some of the steps may happen together, some out of sequence. "Getting it," selling it, trying it, and scaling it often occur almost simultaneously. It is the overall direction that is important, not the sequence.

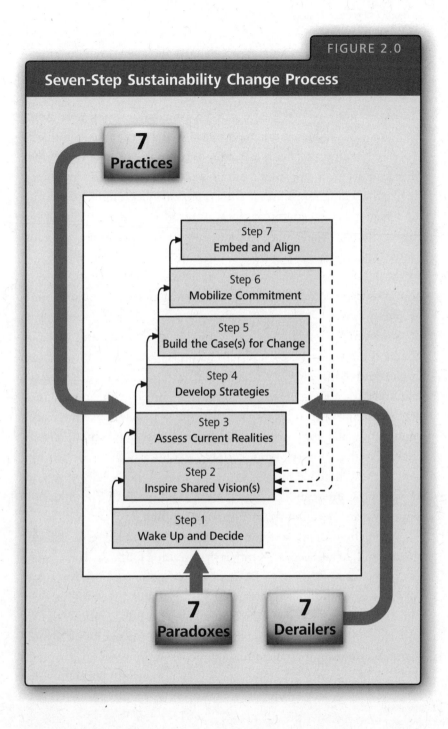

FIGURE 2.0

Seven-Step Sustainability Change Process

7 Practices

Step 7
Embed and Align

Step 6
Mobilize Commitment

Step 5
Build the Case(s) for Change

Step 4
Develop Strategies

Step 3
Assess Current Realities

Step 2
Inspire Shared Vision(s)

Step 1
Wake Up and Decide

7 Paradoxes

7 Derailers

At some point, you become aware of sustainability issues. Your awakening may be gradual as the mainstream media gets better at connecting the dots linking environmental, social, and economic causes and effects, rather than reporting random events. Or your awakening might be like the sudden "spear in the chest" epiphany that Interface CEO Ray Anderson experienced, causing him to recoil from the impacts of his carpet company's take-make-waste corporate model and inspiring his commitment to guide Interface's climb up "Mount Sustainability."[7] It might be a traumatic health event that strikes you or someone close to you, and you become curious about its root causes. Or it could happen another way....

Something happens. Any naïve trust in "the system" and those in charge is forever shattered. You start along Fisher's personal transition curve, outlined in Figure A.1. Sooner or later you get past the denial, fear, and guilt. You decide to channel energy from your anger into a proactive commitment to making a difference — to help make the world more sustainable for yourself, your children, your grandchildren, your friends, your community, your country, and humanity as a whole. You evolve from "someone should" awareness to an "I should" possibility, an "I want to" attitude, an "I can" competence, and an "I will" commitment. Your company becomes your instrument for change.

When circumstances prompt the courage of personal responsibility, the decision to take action — rather than waiting for those who created the problems to fix them — liberates and empowers us. It is invigorating. As you learn about sustainability principles and possibilities, you enter the Awareness stage in the Natural Step's A-B-C-D process shown in Figure 2.1, a condensed four-step reframing of the seven-step organizational sustainability transformation process outlined in this chapter.

FIGURE 2.1

The Natural Step A-B-C-D Change Process

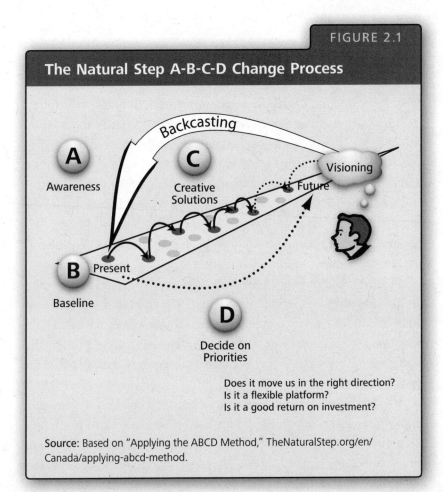

Backcasting

A Awareness

B Present
Baseline

C Creative Solutions

Future

Visioning

D Decide on Priorities

Does it move us in the right direction?
Is it a flexible platform?
Is it a good return on investment?

Source: Based on "Applying the ABCD Method," TheNaturalStep.org/en/Canada/applying-abcd-method.

Shared visions are a continual, open-source work in progress. Creating the future is very different from problem solving. It is not about being less bad; it is about creating the reality you desire. It is not being anti-something; it is being pro-something. A vision portrays a new purpose and aspiration for the company, based on sustainability principles. It is not a passive statement; it is an active, hopeful force. It is not what it says; it is what it does.[8] It is not about having the perfectly worded vision; it is about using the appropriate visioning process to arouse passion and create buy-in. People commit to visions that they help create or reshape.

Begin by using the Big Four Sustainability Challenges and sustainability principles defined by the Natural Step and Natural Capitalism (outlined in Chapter 1) to guide your personal vision of the desired future. You can also use the prompting questions in Figure 2.2 during the visioning process to help craft Big Hairy Audacious Goals (BHAGs) for your chosen sustainability challenge(s).[9]

Repeat the visioning process with an informal network of colleagues who share your sustainability concerns. Everyone may agree to an overarching vision of the company being the most sustainable company in the industry, as assessed by third-party sustainability-ranking organizations like Innovest Strategic Value Advisors. However, sustainability is a holistic concept, so different people will be attracted to different facets of the vision diamond and energized by different aspects of sustainability that are important to them. You may want to brainstorm a portfolio of shared sub-visions of the desired future that individuals can take responsibility for and bring to fruition at their own speed.

People have strong desires to make a difference and leave a legacy. Collective energy, inspiration, and pride from aligned visions/hopes/aspirations will provide the power grid for the exciting change effort ahead.

FIGURE 2.2

Prompts for a Vision of a Sustainable Company

Overall
- If a newspaper featured us as a sustainable company in an article 20 years from now, how would it depict us? What is the article's headline?
- What would our organization look like in a completely sustainable condition 5, 10, or 25 years in the future? How does that future state respect the Natural Step's and Natural Capitalism's principles of sustainability?

Stakeholder Engagement
- What would employees be saying about our company?
- What would external stakeholders be saying about our company? How would we be partnering with them?

Eco-Efficiencies and Product Stewardship
- What would our materials, production, buildings, transportation, energy, waste management, and product stewardship systems look like? Would they be ten times more eco-efficient? Carbon/energy/water neutral? Cradle-to-cradle? Beyond neutral/zero?

Breakthrough Innovations
- What breakthrough sustainable products and services would we be offering? Only leased products? New revenue mix?

Market Expansion
- How would we offer ten times more new products and services in both current and new, underserved markets? What new marketing and distribution systems need to be invented?

Source: Based on Bob Doppelt, *Leading Change toward Sustainability*, Greenleaf Publishing, 2003, p. 135. Some of my own thoughts are interwoven with Doppelt's original suggestions.

Visionary sustainability goals kindle fires in the bellies of colleagues who want to make a difference. To capitalize on their energy, backcast from the exciting future vision to the current reality and assess how large a performance gap exists between the organization's current values, behaviors, offerings, and culture and the desired future state. Use the tension created by that gap to drive action.

A force-field analysis, depicted in Figure 2.2, helps assess current reality by inventorying sustainability drivers and speed-bumps on the organization's sustainability journey. "Forces" could be people inside the organizational hierarchy, external stakeholders, dominant "hot" issues preoccupying people, budget realities, workloads, etc. People are often surprised to discover that some forces are both helping and hindering.

Current reality is not just the "bad news" as opposed to the "good news" of vision statements. Current reality is what we have to work with, just as inventors start with tools and resources at their disposal. By assessing current reality, you gain an overview of the transformational readiness of the company, identifying what you have going for you and what is going against you. You also identify the baseline data you need from such tools as a life-cycle analysis (LCA), carbon footprint calculators, or an annual report on sustainability progress that is aligned with global reporting initiative (GRI) frameworks. These may take time to complete, and you may have to call in outside experts for help, so the assessment usually occurs at the same time as other steps in the sustainability change process.

Encourage people to select a critical subset of helping and hindering forces on which to work. By working on the force field for their favorite sustainability issues, they will propel the company forward on its sustainability journey.

FIGURE 2.3

Force-Field Analysis of Current Reality

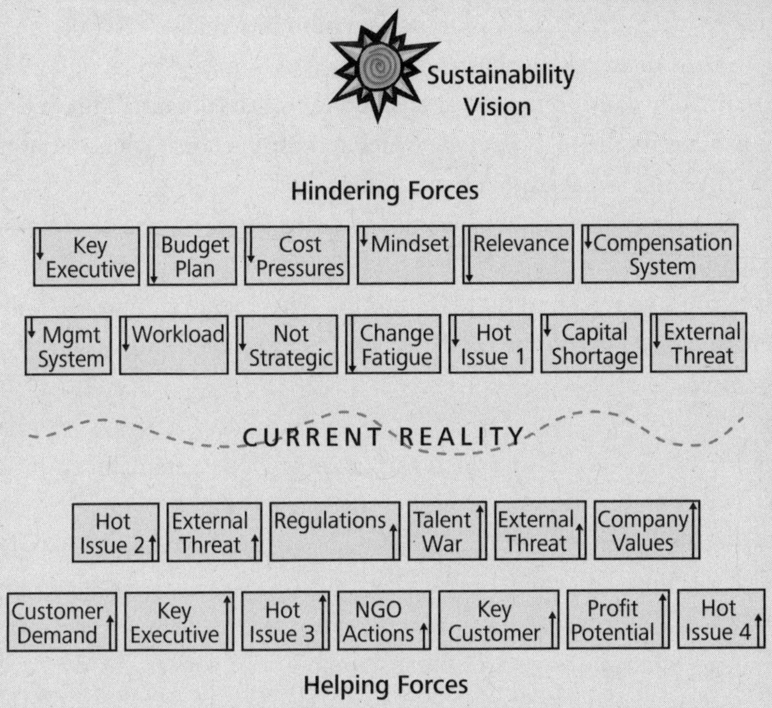

Sustainability
Vision

Hindering Forces

| Key Executive | Budget Plan | Cost Pressures | Mindset | Relevance | Compensation System |

| Mgmt System | Workload | Not Strategic | Change Fatigue | Hot Issue 1 | Capital Shortage | External Threat |

- - - - - - - - - - CURRENT REALITY - - - - - - -

| Hot Issue 2 | External Threat | Regulations | Talent War | External Threat | Company Values |

| Customer Demand | Key Executive | Hot Issue 3 | NGO Actions | Key Customer | Profit Potential | Hot Issue 4 |

Helping Forces

(Arrow length represents the relative strength/importance of the force)

Leadership is the capacity to translate vision into reality.[10] After a force-field assessment reveals the gap between the company's current level of sustainability and your exciting shared vision of its potential future, you must identify the high-leverage issues and those people whose support you need to make it happen.

Relative to the subset of key forces listed in Step 3, think of "leverage points for action," a.k.a. "trigger points," "strategic points of focus," or "strings you need to pull." Determine where you can find the high-leverage trim tabs on the rudder of the organizational ship of state. For example:

- Identify hot issues on which you can piggyback sustainability initiatives
- Recognize customers who are already sustainability allies and who have clout with your company's executives
- List other external stakeholders who your executives respect and who might be advocates for sustainability initiatives, for whatever reason
- Pinpoint influential people in the organization who could accelerate momentum if they championed sustainability initiatives. If they say sustainability is a good idea, everyone will agree.

Leverage points for action are in your Circle of Influence. Your vision, and the key senior executives you need to engage, are in your Circle of Concern. You reach them by expanding your Circle of Influence, as shown in Figure 2.4.

Once you have recognized leverage points for action, brainstorm with your network to identify breakthrough strategies, appropriate metrics, and action plans. Decide who is going to do what, by when, to strengthen helping forces or overcome hindering forces that affect your sustainability vision.

FIGURE 2.4

Use Leverage Points for Action in Your Circle of Influence

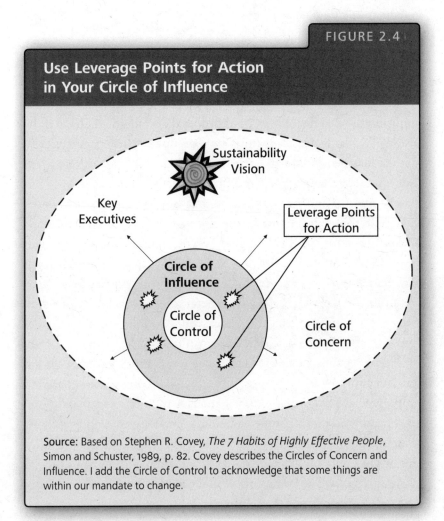

Source: Based on Stephen R. Covey, *The 7 Habits of Highly Effective People*, Simon and Schuster, 1989, p. 82. Covey describes the Circles of Concern and Influence. I add the Circle of Control to acknowledge that some things are within our mandate to change.

Step 5: Build the Case(s) for Change

A critical factor for success is a robust business case that explains how to mitigate risks and quantifies opportunities that could be achieved if the vision of a sustainable company is realized. Just as you generated a port-folio of shared visions in Step 2, now you should build a portfolio of relevant cases for change, tailoring each rationale to your audience.

Use internal and external data to craft compelling justifications for change. It is about becoming a better company, not just a "greener" one.[11] The business case should highlight how your sustainability strategy will improve the bottom line. Use the business language of the department and people you are engaging. Talk about relevant "market forces" and important "stakeholders" that have new expectations about the com-pany's sustainability behaviors. Phrase your case for change in terms of impersonal "risks," "issues," and "opportunities."

Figure 2.5 shows increased employee productivity as the magic en-abler of other benefits. Increased productivity comes from energized employees working smarter, not harder. A move to sustainability in-spires caring, creative people to be peak performers. Employees who share the company's sustainability values and vision are truly its most important asset. They care about environmental and social issues and want the company to be successful so it can be a more positive force in society. They want it to thrive. A sustainability vision inspires employees to improve revenue, think creatively about eco-efficiencies, and ensure innovative products and services are successful.

A compelling, relevant business case convinces others to join the campaign. It builds momentum and helps mobilize commitment.

FIGURE 2.5

Potential Bottom-Line Benefits for a Large Company

	Benefit Area	Improvement
Employee Commitment to Sustainability	1. Reduced recruiting costs	**−1%**
	2. Reduced attrition costs	**−2%**
	3. Increased employee productivity	**+10%**
	4. Eco-efficiencies in manufacturing	**−5%**
	5. Eco-efficiencies at commercial sites	**−20%**
	6. Increased revenue/market share	**+5%**
	7. Lower insurance and borrowing costs	**−5%**

...contributing to a profit increase of at least
+38%

Source: Bob Willard, *The Sustainability Advantage*, New Society Publishers, 2002. The book explains the assumptions and case studies supporting the estimated benefits.

Commitment is mobilized when cross-functional and cross-hierarchical teams collaborate through the steps of the sustainability change process.

Start with your inner circle of kindred spirits. Convene an informal team of like-minded, cross-departmental colleagues who "get" sustainability and have a desire to act. Walk them through Steps 1 to 5 of the seven-step change process (Figure 2.0) and coach them on the stages of team growth shown in Figure 2.6 so that they quickly reach the Performing level.

As they repeat this process with others in their circles of influence, they will earn the collective credibility and influence that will ultimately let them seek support from senior gatekeepers — CEOs, CFOs, board members, and so on — who must give permission for major new initiatives.[12]

Encourage senior gatekeepers to establish a formal, cross-functional senior-level Sustainability Team that has the authority to legitimize the sustainability transformation and be accountable for it. The team's name is not as important as its visible leadership role and clout. Team members are heads of businesses or vice-presidents in key areas who will support and protect sustainability intrapreneurs' efforts to embed sustainability into the mainstream business.[13]

The Sustainability Team sponsors pilot projects and enterprise-wide engagement, education, and collaboration across departmental boundaries to achieve sustainability goals. The team visibly legitimizes the sustainability priority by ensuring progress reports are agenda items in regular senior management meetings. It also guarantees necessary resources are available so all sustainability teams can carry out the "performing" stage.

FIGURE 2.6

Stages of Team Growth

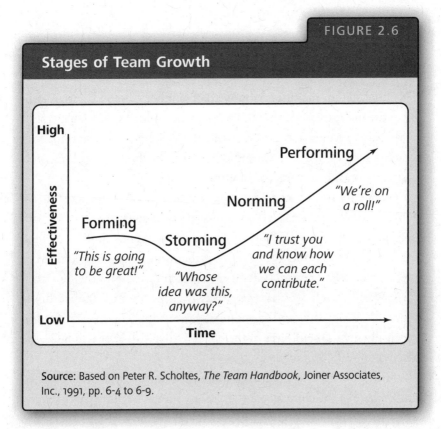

Source: Based on Peter R. Scholtes, *The Team Handbook*, Joiner Associates, Inc., 1991, pp. 6-4 to 6-9.

This final step in the sustainability change process embeds sustainability in the mainstream of the company's measurement and management systems, its recognition and reward systems, and its decision-making systems. Don't leave it to the end of the process, though. Working on it early can significantly increase commitment.

People are too smart to get sucked into another management fad. Most employees have a layer of emotional scar tissue from previous half-baked, flavor-of-the year efforts. They believed the new initiatives were for real, went the extra mile to support them, and then realized that the measurement and reward systems gave them no credit for their good efforts. When people see that executives' rhetoric about sustainability is reflected in how they and the company are evaluated, they will enthusiastically invest themselves in the effort. Otherwise, they will lie in the weeds and wait for it to pass.

As sustainability is gradually integrated into the strategies, policies, and culture of the company, sustainability norms become part of everyone's mindset. Everyone considers the environmental and social impacts of their decisions as they make them. That is the ultimate test of a Stage 4 company: sustainability is embedded in the governance systems and "the way things are done around here," as suggested by the questions in Figure 2.7.

Stay credible. Manage expectations by under-promising and over-delivering on the benefits of sustainability initiatives. Then communicate — the watchword of Step 7. Measure and widely communicate progress on the sustainability journey. Be careful not to "greenwash" and make it all sound like a fait accompli. Rather, celebrate progress toward the new culture, improved business results, and especially any external awards for the company's sustainability leadership.

FIGURE 2.7

Sustainability Alignment Questions

- How will the sustainability culture be reflected in the *measurement, evaluation, and accountability systems?* In the *recognition, reward, and compensation systems?*

- What is the most effective *organizational structure* for getting the work done? Cross-functional teams? Whole units? Networks? Matrix? Individuals?

- What structure enhances *individual, team, and organizational learning* in support of a successful sustainable enterprise?

- What *reporting relationships* are needed to ensure accountability?

- What type of *physical layout* of workstations and office areas will best facilitate learning and implementation while also providing visible, symbolic proof that the company is walking the talk on sustainability?

- What type of governance structure is needed to *generate and share the information* needed to enhance performance toward the sustainability vision and goals?

- What structure is needed to empower employees and stakeholders to *participate in planning and decision making* so that they are energized and committed to contribute their creative ideas to the company's success?

- How will *power and authority relationships* need to change in order to mobilize the whole company and its important stakeholders in support of the sustainable enterprise?

Source: Based on Bob Doppelt, *Leading Change toward Sustainability,* Greenleaf Publishing, 2003, p. 216. Some of my own thoughts are interwoven with Doppelt's original suggestions.

CHAPTER 3

Seven Practices
of Sustainability Champions

There are hundreds of books on how to lead change successfully. In-depth case studies and stories support their guidance. Not surprisingly, the suggestions in one book are echoed in many of the others. This chapter describes seven practices that are most relevant to sustainability champions. As shown in Figure 3.0, these practices apply to all seven steps in the sustainability change process.

These are the dos of sustainability champions — the don'ts are described as derailers in Chapter 5. Are there other sustainability leadership practices that should be included? Undoubtedly. Consider this a high-leverage starter set that will get you 80 percent of the way. Lessons from your own unique experience will take you the rest of the way.

The tone of this and remaining chapters is more prescriptive: do this, do that. The intent is to cut to the chase and share practices that have always worked for effective leaders championing any kind of organizational change. These are the lessons learned — without the backup theory, stories, case studies, and anecdotes.

The seven practices are supplemented by seven paradoxes and seven derailers, explained in the following chapters. Collectively, these three sets of seven are the essence of effective leadership for any organizational culture change, tailored here for the specific transformation to a sustainable enterprise.

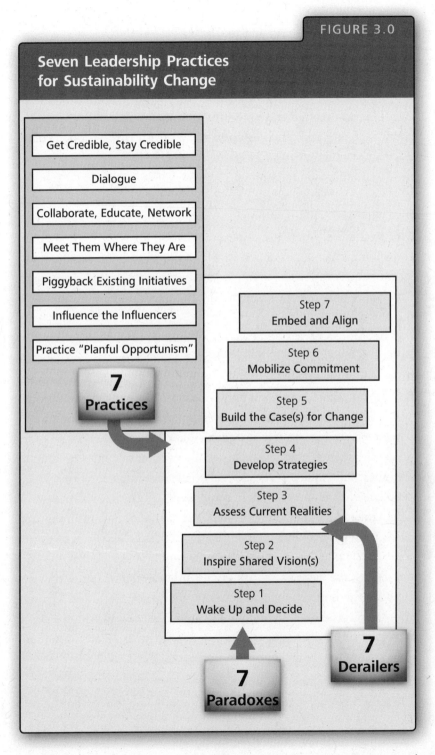

FIGURE 3.0

Seven Leadership Practices for Sustainability Change

Get Credible, Stay Credible

Dialogue

Collaborate, Educate, Network

Meet Them Where They Are

Piggyback Existing Initiatives

Influence the Influencers

Practice "Planful Opportunism"

7 Practices

Step 7
Embed and Align

Step 6
Mobilize Commitment

Step 5
Build the Case(s) for Change

Step 4
Develop Strategies

Step 3
Assess Current Realities

Step 2
Inspire Shared Vision(s)

Step 1
Wake Up and Decide

7 Derailers

7 Paradoxes

It is important to establish your personal credibility early on. You must earn the right to lead the sustainability transformation. Leadership is about influence and relationships based on trust. Trustworthy, credible leaders are honest, forward-looking, inspiring, and competent.[14] You need to build trust quickly.

Figure 3.1 shows how trustworthiness is the foundation of credible leadership and is based on both competence and character. Character is hard to change. If you don't have a reputation for being an honest, incorruptible, ethical, caring person who walks the talk on sustainability, seriously question whether you are the best person to lead the change. Charlatans who lead the sustainability change process are not good for the cause.

The competence aspect of credibility is easier to address. You need to have three kinds of credibility: credibility as a champion of sustainability, credibility as a leader of change, and credibility as a business leader. Become an expert in the first two — sustainability and organizational leadership — the same way you develop personal mastery in any discipline: read, study, reflect, listen, practice, and network. Keep up to date on developments in your industry while gaining an understanding of relevant sustainability issues and potentially innovative solutions. When people see you as an experienced center of expertise, they will trust your judgment and competence to lead the sustainability transformation.[15]

As for the third kind of credibility, executives especially need to feel comfortable that you are an authentic business leader — that you will not suggest the company adopt sustainability strategies unless they are good for the bottom line and enhance stock value. You need to assert your business acumen frequently. Otherwise, executives will be uneasy that your sustainability agenda is not aligned with — and is perhaps even a threat to — the company's success.

FIGURE 3.1

Principle-Centered Leadership

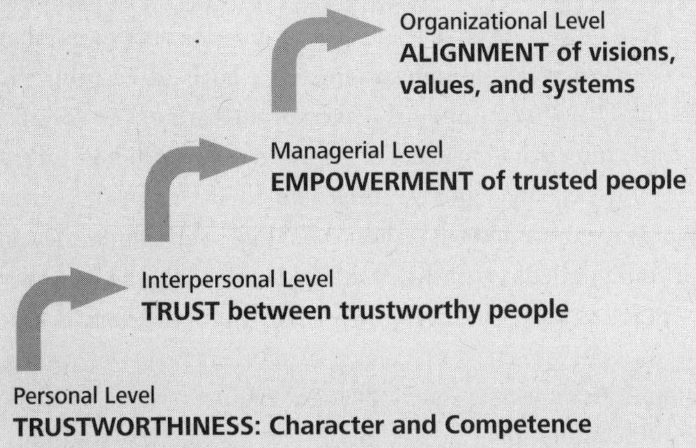

Organizational Level
ALIGNMENT of visions, values, and systems

Managerial Level
EMPOWERMENT of trusted people

Interpersonal Level
TRUST between trustworthy people

Personal Level
TRUSTWORTHINESS: Character and Competence

Source: Based on ideas about conditions of empowerment in Stephen R. Covey, A. Roger Merrill and Rebecca R. Merrill, *First Things First*, Simon and Schuster, 1994, pp. 238–44.

Developing persuasion/selling skills that allow you to influence others makes you a more effective leader.[16] You must be able to use dialogue to advocate for breakthrough sustainability goals and a culture of sustainability. Dialogue reminds us that communication is a two-way street with many interesting intersections, not a one-way, dead-end alley.

People, especially senior executives, do not like to be told what to do. They prefer to be asked what should be done. Sometimes they are uneasy if your good idea is one they should have had themselves; they may feel compelled to save face by showing why yours will not work. The secret to influencing senior managers — influencing anyone, actually — is dialogue. As Figure 3.2 shows, dialogue requires the leader to inquire, listen, respectfully advocate a point of view, and propose solutions. True generative dialogue does not "smooth over" the issue for polite agreement. It requires you to suspend assumptions, reflect on your own and others' ingrained mental models, and balance advocacy with inquiry.[17]

People in dialogue need to make their assumptions explicit through questions such as "Can you help me understand how you see sustainability differently?" or "What are the assumptions behind your conclusion?"[18]

Mastering the art of effective conversation will help sustainability champions negotiate effectively with opposers. Through dialogue, others will see that a sustainable approach is not at odds with corporate purposes and objectives. By listening to and acknowledging other's perspectives, you make sure everyone feels valued and you generate new possibilities based on shared meaning. Focusing on interests and assumptions rather than personal positions will spark win-win outcomes that all parties will value.[19] The journey to success can take more than one route.[20] Dialogue helps find the best one for everyone.

FIGURE 3.2

Dialogue Balances Advocacy and Inquiry

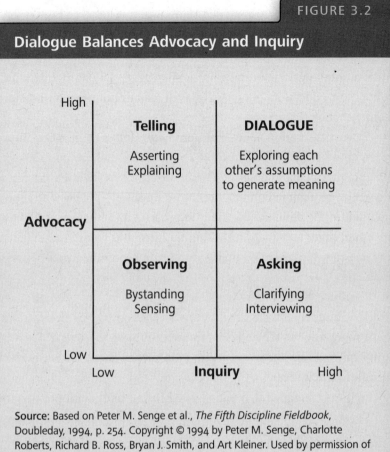

Source: Based on Peter M. Senge et al., *The Fifth Discipline Fieldbook*, Doubleday, 1994, p. 254. Copyright © 1994 by Peter M. Senge, Charlotte Roberts, Richard B. Ross, Bryan J. Smith, and Art Kleiner. Used by permission of Doubleday, a division of Random House, Inc.

3. Collaborate, Educate, Network

If "location, location, location" is the mantra of real estate agents, "collaboration, education, networking" is the mantra of successful sustainability change champions.

True collaboration is not prevalent within most companies. Too often, departments find themselves in dysfunctional competition with other departments. People collaborate when it is in their self-interest to do so, so you want to connect peers with purpose.[21] People who share a compelling vision of the company as a sustainable enterprise will work together, share resources, reallocate budgets, and contribute expertise because they want to make their common dreams come true. They need each other's help and connections to make it happen.

Convince the company to educate employees and external stakeholders about what sustainability is, what the company is already doing to be more responsible and why, and what it plans to do next. Then ask employees to help the company go even farther, faster. Empower them to unleash their ideas.

Figure 3.3 suggests that you not only collaborate with networks of colleagues in your department and other departments, but also with enlightened customers whose voices are respected in your executive suite and with non-governmental organizations (NGOs) and governmental agencies whose profile can add credibility to your efforts. Sustainability culture change arises from a wonderfully chaotic, self-organizing network of alliances that evolve from your node of kindred spirits. These early-adopter sustainability emissaries cause a ripple effect in their multiple networks that creates an undercurrent of committed colleagues, accelerating the sustainability transformation as the waves reach the upper echelons of the organization and cascade throughout the organization.

FIGURE 3.3

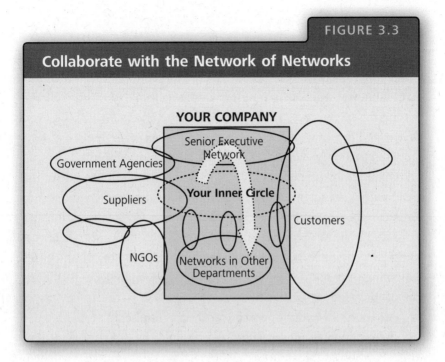

Collaborate with the Network of Networks

YOUR COMPANY

Senior Executive Network

Government Agencies

Suppliers

Your Inner Circle

Customers

NGOs

Networks in Other Departments

4. Meet Them Where They Are

Inevitably, you will face opposition. Opposers think your proposals are wrong for the business and/or wrong for them personally. When you confront different worldviews, talk the jargon of the opposers and show how sustainability strategies are relevant to their priorities.[22]

Leave it to external activists to whack executives on the side of the head with wake-up accusations. As an inside salesperson, you need to protect opposers' credibility and help them save face. Cooperation and conflict resolution will pay off enormously the next time you meet them, which you will. Emphasize "new news," and help opposers see emerging risks and opportunities from rising stakeholder expectations about company sustainability.

Put yourself in your opposers' shoes and mindset. Assume they are good, smart people who feel compelled to play by capitalism's current rules. Position sustainability as a set of enabling strategies that will help them meet existing goals, not as one more goal to worry about. Different risks and benefits will resonate with different managers and executives depending on their roles, interests, measurements, aspirations, and priorities. Honor them. Meet them where they are, use their terminology, and appeal to their interests. Use their assumptions, data, and experience to quantify relevant potential financial benefits using business case spreadsheets. Make the business case theirs, not yours.[23]

Pay attention to intangibles and values-based motivations. In a business context, these are not usually allowed to be the sole rationale for sustainability actions, but they do help stimulate a desire to find sufficient quantifiable, material, and economic "business" justification for sustainability actions that people already want to take for the "right reasons."

FIGURE 3.4

Meet Them Where They Are — Be Relevant

- When talking to *Sales Managers,* start by mentioning exciting new revenue streams from creatively breaking into underserved markets at the Base of the Pyramid (BOP) of the world's population or potential top-line revenue increases from an enhanced sustainability reputation and offerings.

- When talking to *Human Resources Managers,* lead with a description of how the company's improved corporate social responsibility image will help win the War for Talent, mitigate attrition of key people, and motivate employees.

- When talking to *Production or Manufacturing Managers,* the best hook may be your explanation of how sustainability will secure materials, energy, or water supply; achieve eco-efficiencies; or help them with their increasing accountability for environmental and social impacts in the supply chain.

- When talking to *Finance Managers,* emphasize overall bottom-line benefits and institutional investors' and bankers' awakened interest in how the company is addressing its sustainability-related risks.

5. Piggyback Existing Initiatives

People are way too busy to welcome one more thing to worry about. In some companies, hitching your sustainability wagon to an existing high-profile horse will help move it in the right direction. Wherever possible, use existing processes. This allows easy access to company resources and know-how, and helps create support by getting more of the mainstream company involved.

If there is already a strong focus on Total Quality Management (TQM) or Lean Manufacturing in the company, sustainability is a close cousin. It is about reducing waste, improving efficiencies, engaging with stakeholders — especially customers — and integrating those priorities into management systems. ISO 9000 for quality management and ISO 14000 for environmental management systems have much in common. The much-awaited ISO 26000 guidance document for corporate social responsibility may provide another coat-tail to ride on.

Similarly, if the corporate culture already includes a high-profile focus on environment, health, and safety (EHS), piggyback on that legitimacy. Expand it into a more holistic sustainability effort by partnering with the community relations department; then help both departments leap the "green wall" that may be marginalizing their contributions from mainline business strategies.

Aligning with revered priorities will reinforce the idea that sustainability aligns with the company values, purpose, mission, and beliefs; it connects with the generative corporate DNA. Avoid the temptation to reinvent the wheel — the vehicle for change may already be at hand. Piggyback on current, high-visibility programs to accelerate and expedite the sustainability journey (see examples of good candidates in Figure 3.5).

FIGURE 3.5

Good Piggyback Candidates

- Environment, Health, and Safety (EHS)

- Total Quality Management (TQM)

- Six Sigma

- Lean Manufacturing

- Community Relations

- Philanthropy

- Diversity Programs

It is nearly impossible to accomplish a transformation to a sustainability culture without long-term buy-in and active support from a majority of the network of formal and informal power brokers in the organization. Companies tend to respond energetically to signals from the CEO and other senior executives, so the formation of a high-level Sustainability Team is a strategic priority to mobilize commitment. For sustainability champions without position power, that may seem like bad news.

The good news is that you can work the chain of influence leading to the key people. Use the "Collaborate, Educate, Network" practice. Start with your network of kindred spirits and their contacts; then collaboratively find paths through the chain of influence that connects to senior gatekeepers, as suggested by the effective approach depicted in Figure 3.6.

Set aside the official hierarchical/positional organization chart and compose a relationship/network chart so you can identify who is in the inner circle of those whose support is critical to your sustainability efforts. Perform this due diligence early so that you know who is on the periphery and who "counts." Do certain people have the ability to get senior support for the sustainability transformation? If so, cultivate them so they will be comfortable influencing others in their influence chain.

People listen to people they know and trust. Work your network so you avoid hurling a plea over the transom at a senior executive who doesn't know you and is too busy to bother understanding what a stranger wants. Find those influencers of executives; influence them to be your advocates.

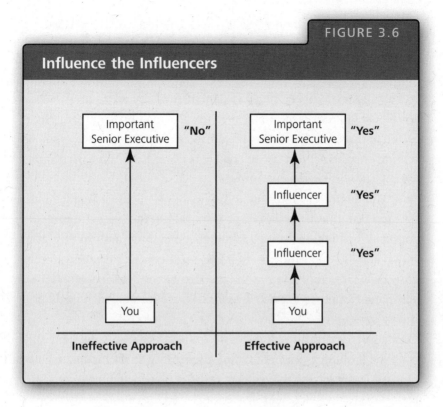

FIGURE 3.6

Influence the Influencers

Ineffective Approach | **Effective Approach**

7. Practice "Planful Opportunism"

It is all about timing. Be urgently patient and be ready to capitalize on triggers of interest. Become an expert on sustainability and change leadership so that when external market forces demand senior executives' attention to sustainability issues, you are ready to help. You have planned for it. Capitalize on the opportunity.

If you attempt to integrate a sustainability initiative into the business at a bad time, or in the wrong way, you run the risk of diluting impact and burning bridges. People need different stimuli to buy in to an agenda. Be opportunistic and adapt to new circumstances as they arise. Be flexible about timing and paths to success, but do not budge on achieving real progress toward your visionary sustainability goals (Figure 3.7).

Planful opportunism does not mean sitting on your hands and waiting for a flashing green light before proceeding. It means creating opportunities by having the courage to let it be widely known that you are a knowledgeable, credible person who cares about sustainability and its value as a strategic enabler of company success. Strangely, once word spreads that you are creating a sustainability groundswell, you will become a lightning rod for people who need help with sustainability-related issues. Be ready for those serendipitous and teachable moments. Capitalize on the goodwill and support you will earn by being helpful.

Finally, planful opportunism is about scalability. We need to pilot sustainability solutions that are rapidly scalable in the company, in the industry, in other industries, and in other countries. The demand for sustainable solutions is exploding. Prepare your company to planfully capitalize on those opportunities.

FIGURE 3.7

Jack Welch's "Planful Opportunism" Strategy

Perhaps the most important idea [Jack Welch, CEO of General Electric] developed in those days is what I call "planful opportunism." Instead of directing a business according to a detailed GE-style strategic plan, Welch believed in setting a few, clear overarching goals. Then, on an ad hoc basis, his people were free to seize any opportunities they saw to further those goals.

Welch operated that way instinctively, but the notion crystallized in his mind in the late 1970s after he read Johannes van Moltke, a nineteenth-century Prussian general influenced by the renowned military theorist Karl von Clausewitz. Von Moltke argued that detailed plans usually fail, because circumstances inevitably change. A successful strategist, he wrote, always must be willing to adapt; even broad goals must be flexible enough to respond to new events.

Source: Noel M. Tichy and Stratford Sherman, *Control Your Destiny or Someone Else Will,* Doubleday, 1993, p. 52. Copyright © 1993 by Noel M. Tichy and Stratford Sherman. Used by permission of Doubleday, a division of Random House, Inc.

CHAPTER 4

Seven Paradoxes to Use

- Introduction

- You Have to Do It Yourself; You Can't Do It Alone

- To Get "Hard Results," Work on the "Soft Stuff"

- Motivators Inhibit Commitment

- One Person's Dream Is Another Person's Nightmare

- Go Slow to Go Fast

- Go Small to Go Big

- Things Need to Get Worse Before They Can Get Better

The seven paradoxes used by successful sustainability champions reinforce each other, and they all reinforce the seven practices. Because they seem to contradict themselves, the paradoxes may be more memorable than the seven practices.

Although not listed as one of the seven paradoxes, "less is more," or "less yields more," is an umbrella paradox that applies to the others.

PARADOX	"LESS YIELDS MORE" VERSION
You have to do it yourself; you can't do it alone[24]	Less push by you yields more push by others
To get "hard results," work on the "soft stuff"	A less aggressive style yields more aggressive results
Motivators inhibit commitment	Less/fewer rewards yield more motivation
One person's dream is another person's nightmare	Less selling yields more sales
Go slow to go fast	Less rush yields faster results
Go small to go big	Less splash yields bigger waves
Things need to get worse before they can get better	Less readiness yields better readiness

As you read about sustainability leadership paradoxes in this chapter, I expect you will discover more of your own. Is that another paradox...?

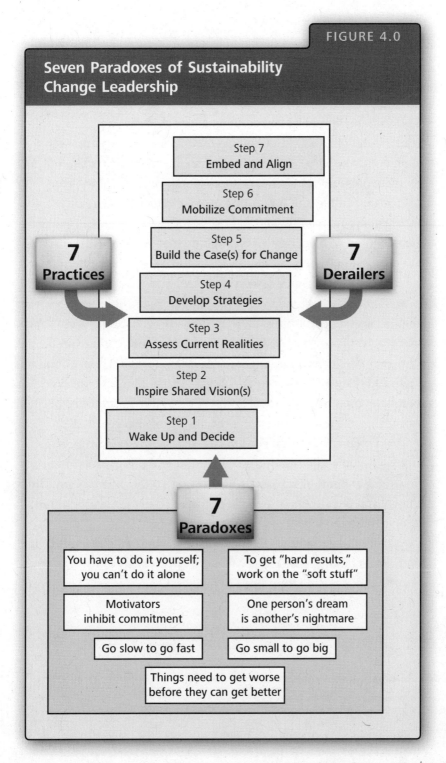

FIGURE 4.0

Seven Paradoxes of Sustainability Change Leadership

7 Practices

7 Derailers

Step 7
Embed and Align

Step 6
Mobilize Commitment

Step 5
Build the Case(s) for Change

Step 4
Develop Strategies

Step 3
Assess Current Realities

Step 2
Inspire Shared Vision(s)

Step 1
Wake Up and Decide

7 Paradoxes

You have to do it yourself; you can't do it alone	To get "hard results," work on the "soft stuff"
Motivators inhibit commitment	One person's dream is another's nightmare
Go slow to go fast	Go small to go big
Things need to get worse before they can get better	

1. You Have to Do It Yourself; You Can't Do It Alone

Although most intrapreneurs are comfortable acting as lone wolves at least some of the time, sustainability champions need to be effective team leaders. Their energy, vision, courage, and relentless optimism keep the momentum building. Sometimes they are the marquee leader, convening networks and sub-networks. Or they may be the behind-the-scenes leader, applauding and supporting other leaders who share their commitment to sustainability and expanding the ripple effect of sustainability initiatives. As sustainability champions, they are the catalysts making the change to a sustainable enterprise happen — through others.

The irony of personal leadership is that you must inspire and empower others to move your vision forward. Engaging other stakeholders requires listening, learning, and building shared commitments. These skills are at the heart of effective leadership. You need others' ideas, energy, resources, and commitment to trigger the series of springboards in Figure 4.1 that enable your sustainability dreams. Margaret Mead said it best: "Never doubt that a small group of thoughtful, committed people can change the world. Indeed, it is the only thing that ever has."[25]

Understand the critical need to engage others to achieve buy-in. Action on sustainability requires collaboration, and effective intrapreneurs are adept at building coalitions with others in the organization. Ultimately, you must share ownership of sustainability initiatives with key people throughout your organization.

Leadership encourages people to share the burden of responsibility and accountability. Giving away ownership of sustainability programs to others in the company is not a sign of weakness; it is a sign of leadership.

FIGURE 4.1

If I Had a Lever Long Enough...

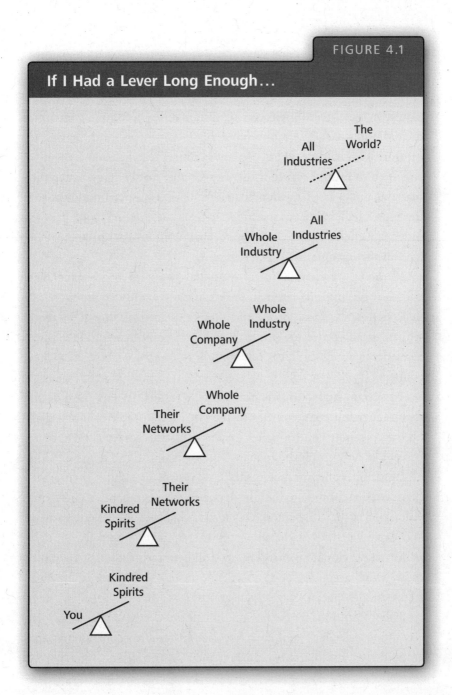

2. To Get "Hard Results," Work on the "Soft Stuff"

Consider the three dimensions of sustainability: economic, environmental, and social. The economic/financial dimension is the easiest to measure with hard numbers. The environmental dimension is the next easiest to measure because it involves savings from energy, water, raw material, and waste-handling eco-efficiencies. The social dimension is the most challenging to quantify. The irony is that the "soft" people-oriented benefits are the most important. Without energized, productive, inspired people, not much happens.

Figure 3.2 represents a typical seven-dial corporate control panel. The company responds to external market forces by adjusting three "hard" dials/factors: business goals and strategies; organizational systems, structures, and processes; products and services. Enhancing these three elements is necessary but is not enough to create a high-performance company.

To sustain high-performance business results, leaders must apply their leadership competencies to the two "soft" people-oriented dials on the corporate control panel. Leadership styles account for 50 to 70 percent of how employees perceive their organization's climate.[26] The organizational climate determines how people feel about themselves, their work environment, their leaders, and their company. An inspiring vision of a sustainable enterprise elevates the level of energy, creativity, and capability they will voluntarily invest in the company. A high-performance climate contributes to employee satisfaction and productivity, which accounts for 20 to 30 percent of the variance in business results of high-performing organizations over others.[27]

The soft stuff makes the hard stuff happen. That's why sustainability champions need leadership practices that invigorate a collaborative and empowering sustainability culture in their organization.

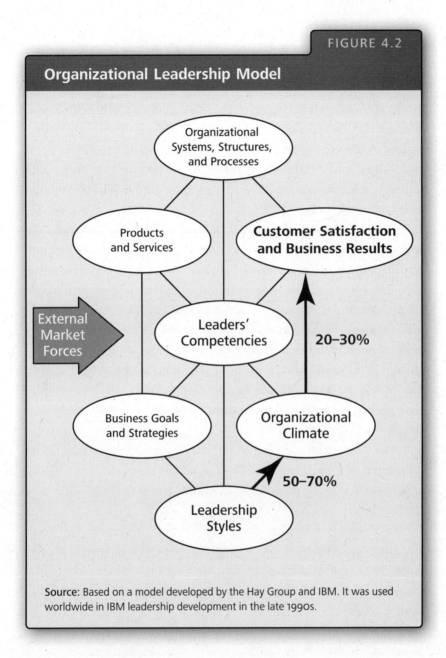

FIGURE 4.2

Organizational Leadership Model

Organizational Systems, Structures, and Processes

Products and Services

Customer Satisfaction and Business Results

External Market Forces

Leaders' Competencies

20–30%

Business Goals and Strategies

Organizational Climate

50–70%

Leadership Styles

Source: Based on a model developed by the Hay Group and IBM. It was used worldwide in IBM leadership development in the late 1990s.

Although managers are sometimes encouraged to motivate their employees, the irony is that they cannot. In reality, extrinsic rewards like money and parties produce short-term hygiene rather than long-term motivation. And if extrinsic motivators require people to compete with colleagues for the motivator/prize, they may inhibit intrinsic motivation and commitment to the task.[28]

People decide when they will be truly motivated. They hold the unique key that unlocks their own enthusiasm, wisdom, creative ideas, and productivity. They are intrinsically self-motivated by something they care about. Sustainability is a wonderful catalyst for self-motivation.

Others cannot commit you to sustainability initiatives; you voluntarily commit yourself when you wake up and decide to make a difference. Figure 4.3 shows the four ingredients in the recipe for commitment: clarity of the goal; relevance to the business's success and your role in it; involvement in shaping the plan (which makes you feel valued, trusted, and respected); and meaning that resonates with your deeply held personal values.

Involvement and meaning are the magic ingredients. Sustainability intrapreneurs foster commitment to sustainability strategies by involving others in shaping them. They allow others to plan the battle so they will not battle the plan.

Sustainability initiatives thrive on meaning. When corporate values align with personal values, employee energy, creativity, and commitment are unleashed, accelerating sustainability changes and adding passion capital to the financial, natural, and social capitals of sustainability.

Compliance requires the first two ingredients; commitment needs all four. Compliance is extrinsically motivated obedience; commitment is an intrinsically motivated personal pledge.

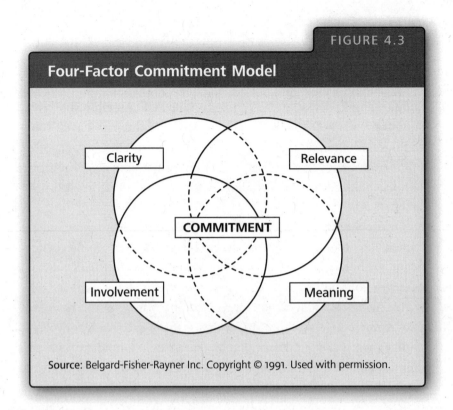

Suppose you have worked for 20 years on the SUV assembly line in an automotive plant. A "greenie" shares her sustainability vision with you: communities built around public transportation and car-sharing pools of super-efficient vehicles. That shift in consumer preferences and behaviors could put you out of a job. Is that a good thing for you personally?

Or suppose you are an executive whose ego and identity are intertwined with your title in the corporate hierarchy. Your self-esteem depends on how your executive compensation compares with that of others in your golf foursome. A "tree hugger" employee excitedly describes his sustainability vision for your company, including egalitarian, non-hierarchical governance approaches. Is that a good thing for you?

As others hear your description of a sustainable future, they race up their ladder of inference, depicted in Figure 4.4. They filter what you say through their beliefs and assumptions about you, sustainability issues, their security, the company, and the world. As they reach the top rung, they may have quickly and quietly concluded something very different from what you intended.

Anticipate the personal implications of your sustainability vision for those whose support you are seeking. Solicit feedback and reactions from them so that you become sensitive to their interpretations. Be careful about how quickly and completely you sell your sustainability vision. Use the KISS approach — keep it simple, stupid — especially at first. Do a slow reveal that gently pulls people along their personal sustainability journeys at their own pace. This will allow them to embrace the associated self-chosen and self-empowering personal transitions rather than rejecting them as personal threats.

FIGURE 4.4

The Ladder of Inference

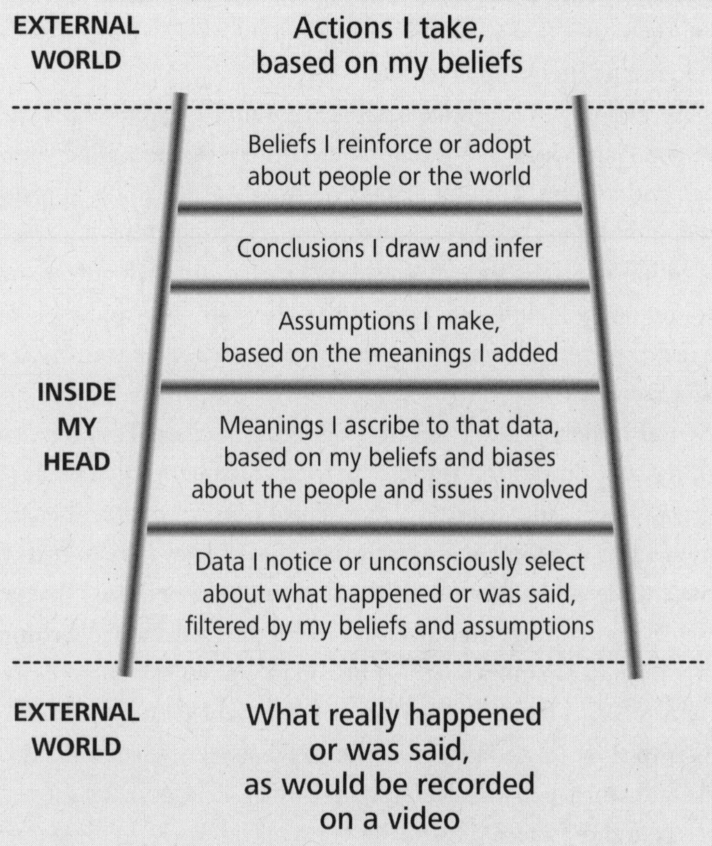
EXTERNAL WORLD
Actions I take, based on my beliefs
Beliefs I reinforce or adopt about people or the world
Conclusions I draw and infer
Assumptions I make, based on the meanings I added
INSIDE MY HEAD
Meanings I ascribe to that data, based on my beliefs and biases about the people and issues involved
Data I notice or unconsciously select about what happened or was said, filtered by my beliefs and assumptions
EXTERNAL WORLD
What really happened or was said, as would be recorded on a video

Source: Based on Peter M. Senge et al., *The Fifth Discipline Fieldbook*, Doubleday, 1994, p. 243. Copyright © 1994 by Peter M. Senge, Charlotte Roberts, Richard B. Ross, Bryan J. Smith, and Art Kleiner. Used by permission of Doubleday, a division of Random House, Inc.

A profound sense of urgency about environmental issues like climate change can cause sustainability change agents to become strident zealots. Do not let that happen to you.

Give people time to wake up to sustainability at a pace that works for them. Plant seeds, ask questions, alert them to relevant new market forces, and coach them along their personal sustainability journey so they do not dig in their heels and disconnect. Listen, learn, engage, and then propose. This is the art of leading change and dialogue. If you try to go too fast, you will lose them. When the stars align and their readiness factor is right, they will get it on their own and be your most supportive converts.

Senior leaders pride themselves on being decisive. They have to be. Their days are time-sliced among a myriad of issues brought to them for approval, advice, and decision. They do not have time to deliberate and study matters as completely as they would like. They have to trust their instincts and decide. That is why they are paid the big bucks. That is also why they may confuse their decision to become a sustainable company with achieving organization-wide buy-in to that vision. Then they wonder why it is so difficult to mobilize commitment to their vision.

Going slow to go fast closes the gap between when a decision is made and when people affected by it buy in. As Figure 4.5 shows, giving a say to those affected by the decision may delay its implementation a little. However, the benefit of this approach is that it gives people a chance to build personal commitment and take ownership of initiatives because they helped shape them. Their slower collective decision is concurrent with their faster buy-in.

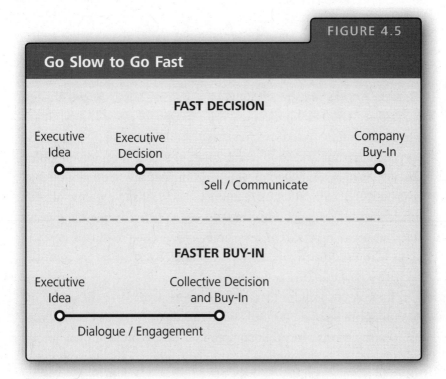

6. Go Small to Go Big

How do you eat an elephant? One bite at a time. How do you change a company? One pilot project at a time. Successful pilots and symbolic acts are important milestones for sustainability strategies.

Small startup endeavors seem to be the best jumping-off point for any changemaker. Design timely prototypes that are practical and scalable. Start with pilots that capture the low-hanging fruit of eco-efficiencies before going big. This allows you to experiment and learn while minimizing risks. For companies with limited resources, partnerships with third parties like universities and NGOs can be useful incubators for new thinking and initiatives.[29]

Pilots are cocoons for ideas. They reassure people that disruptive innovations can be taken seriously without jeopardizing the needs of customers who contribute profit and growth.[30] Pilots provide a safe "proof of concept" lab and show how you can collaborate across departmental and hierarchical boundaries. Choose areas where conditions are favorable for successfully incubating sustainability solutions that add value to both society and the bottom line. Build contingency plans, and protect credibility by not overstating the results. Look for early, small wins that snowball. These will build company enthusiasm to scale up the incubated projects, propelling them into the mainstream.

Symbolic acts also have big effects. You might hire a high-profile senior executive from the outside who "gets" sustainability, visibly reward and promote employees who walk the talk on sustainability, use hydrids as company cars, or install skylights to enhance employee well-being while saving energy.[31] Micro-changes add up to macro-changes and, as the ripple effect in Figure 4.6 suggests, small moves produce big shifts.[32]

FIGURE 4.6

The Ripple Effect

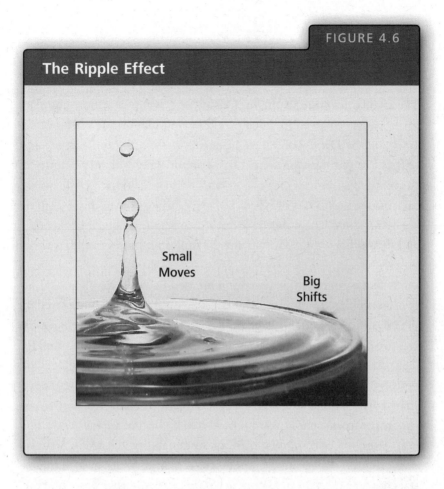

Small
Moves

Big
Shifts

The change literature is unanimous on one premise: a "burning platform" causes change. The idea of a "burning platform" comes from a story told by Daryl Conner in *Managing at the Speed of Change.*[33] He tells of a nighttime explosion and fire on the Piper Alfa oil platform in the North Sea, off the coast of Scotland, on July 6, 1988. It was the worst catastrophe in 25 years of North Sea exploration. One of the few survivors, Andy Mochan, plunged 150 feet (15 stories) into a burning sea of oil and debris, knowing he would survive only 20 minutes in the freezing water.

Why did Andy jump? When interviewed in the hospital, he said he chose uncertain death over certain death — he knew that if he stayed in the inferno on the platform, he would die. The pain of his current reality was too great. He jumped because he had to, not because he wanted to.

Personal and organizational change is often precipitated by a real or perceived "burning platform." It helps to have the pull of an attractive shared vision. But change is usually pushed by discomfort with the status quo or unease about what is predicted if changes are not made. For executives, the burning platform for sustainability will likely be business-oriented risks from a confluence of market forces and changing stakeholder expectations about corporate social and environmental impacts.

Actually, it is better to have a burning platform situation than the boiled frog syndrome, in which the victim awakens to the danger too late to recover (Figure 4.7). Sustainability champions can alert executives to the sustainability-related threats menacing the company and explain how sustainability strategies will help turn down the heat under the corporate pot.

FIGURE 4.7

The Boiled Frog Syndrome

Scientific research has discovered that *frogs cannot perceive an increase in surrounding water temperature if the water is heated gently so that the increase is slow and steady.* Eventually the frog dies, still unaware of the threat it faces.

MarketWatch has reported that a panel of experts at the World Economic Forum's meeting in Davos have warned the organization that "international corporations suffer from boiling frog syndrome" and are "in denial about the daunting array of risks they face, including terrorism, disease pandemics, climate change and a potential Chinese economic slowdown."

"Corporations...all-too-often plan only for the risks they already know about," MarketWatch reports panellists saying. "Unfortunately, there is a widespread tendency among many businesses to be well prepared only for the last event that has occurred — not the next one coming around the corner," the panel wrote in its report to the World Economic Forum. "Denial is an all-too-common strategy, and *there is a natural tendency not to react until the catastrophe is unavoidable.*"

Panel members called on businesses and political leaders to think innovatively about how to face down the growing array of risks and warned that *without new approaches, the dangers would grow.*

Source: "World Economic Forum warned about 'boiling frog' syndrome," Continuity Central website, January 28, 2005 (continuitycentral.com/news01723 .htm) (italics added).

CHAPTER 5

Seven Derailers to Avoid

Two kinds of speed bumps can derail your sustainability efforts: obstacles in your Circle of Concern, like a severe economic downturn or a natural disaster disrupting the company's supply chain; and impediments in your Circle of Influence (see Figure 2.4).

The derailers outlined in this chapter are ones you can control or influence, like your personal behavior and others' perception of it. In other words, you can control how you lead your company's sustainability revolution.

There are many ways to screw up organizational change. The seven described here are a subset of Egger's "Top Ten Executive Derailment Factors."[34] In case you are curious, the three dropped from Egger's original list are:

- "Alienating Your Boss," which is encompassed by "Mishandling Office Politics"
- "Over-Reliance on a Mentor," which has more to do with derailing career advancement than derailing organizational change
- "Suffering from a Bad Image," which is embedded in "Being a Problem Child" and "Displaying Hubris"

Seven are enough decelerators to worry about.

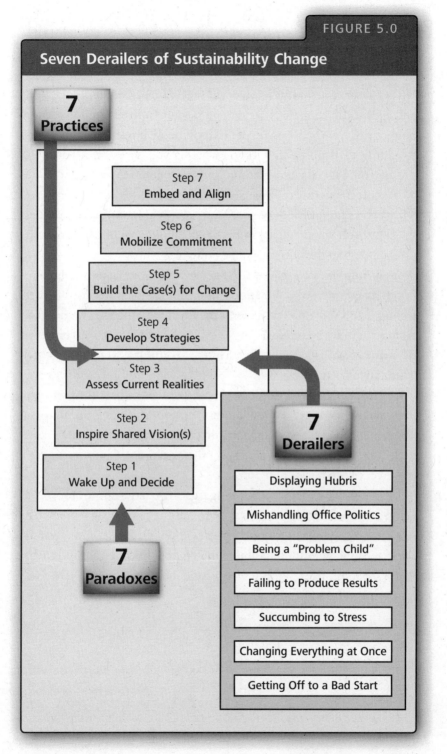

FIGURE 5.0

Seven Derailers of Sustainability Change

7 Practices

Step 7
Embed and Align

Step 6
Mobilize Commitment

Step 5
Build the Case(s) for Change

Step 4
Develop Strategies

Step 3
Assess Current Realities

Step 2
Inspire Shared Vision(s)

Step 1
Wake Up and Decide

7 Paradoxes

7 Derailers

Displaying Hubris

Mishandling Office Politics

Being a "Problem Child"

Failing to Produce Results

Succumbing to Stress

Changing Everything at Once

Getting Off to a Bad Start

No one likes an arrogant "know-it-all." If you are perceived as cold, aloof, and egotistical, your effectiveness as a sustainability champion is exponentially diminished. Even if you start off being humble, if success goes to your head, people will question whether you have always had a hidden personal agenda, career ambitions, and a desire to look good.

Reflect frequently on what you are doing, how you are doing it, and what others might think of you. Your "personal brand" is what others say about you when you are not around. Being authentic improves the probability that the hearsay will be positive.

Stay humble (see Figure 5.1). Be generous in your acknowledgments of others' efforts. Avoid presenting your ideas as the only answer. Invite feedback and stay open to better ideas from other people. Rather than taking yourself too seriously, make yourself vulnerable to learning better ways of leading sustainability. Think of yourself as a facilitator/coach instead of a guru/hero.

Ask for advice. Few people can resist the urge to share their wisdom. Seek executives' ideas on how best to accomplish the significant organizational and cultural change required to become a sustainable enterprise. Take notes to show you respect their opinions. Consider asking a key executive to be your mentor.

Leading change is about building trusting relationships. Hubris and ego destroy relationships. Show genuine caring for colleagues and their sustainability efforts, with many goodwill deposits in their emotional bank accounts.[35] Adopt an abundance mentality and give away what you want most: trust, respect, recognition, help, and support. They will return a hundredfold.

FIGURE 5.1

Quotations about Humility

Humility does not mean thinking less of yourself than of other people, nor does it mean having a low opinion of your own gifts. It means freedom from thinking about yourself at all.

— Sir William Temple (1881–1944)

A man wrapped up in himself makes a very small bundle.

— Benjamin Franklin (1706–1790)

If I only had a little humility, I would be perfect.

— Ted Turner (1938–)

True merit is like a river: the deeper it is, the less noise it makes.

—Edward Frederick Lindley Wood, 1st Earl of Halifax (1881–1959)

Egotism is the anesthetic that dulls the pain of stupidity.

Frank Leahy (1908–1973)

None are so empty as those who are full of themselves.

Benjamin Whichcote (1609–1683)

Source: Terri Guillemets, Quote Garden website (quotegarden.com/humility .html).

Messing up on office politics can be a career-limiting and change-limiting move. It is bad for you and it is bad for the sustainability cause.

The first way to mishandle office politics is closely associated with hubris, described above. You consciously — or otherwise — take credit for colleagues' accomplishments and ideas, alienating those who sense you are clambering over them to garner favor with management. This is the kiss of death for vital relationships in your carefully built network of sustainability co-champions and makes your efforts look like they are about earning brownie points for yourself rather than about sustainability and the company's success.

The second way to mishandle office politics is to make managers — either the manager to whom you report or others — look bad. Managers may initially resist your ideas because accepting the sustainability changes you advocate would force them to indict their past decisions and behaviors. You need to be politically savvy, using carefully honed diplomatic and political skills to avoid betraying mangers' trust. Make deposits to their emotional bank accounts, not withdrawals (Figure 5.2). If a manager is an opposer, be careful about doing an end run and secretly calling above him for support. That tactic will further alienate the manager and may change him from a passive opposer to an active disparager.

Especially do not badmouth unsupportive managers behind their backs. Backstabbing is like a boomerang. Instead, dialogue with them. Gently shed light on the assumptions that support your different points of view. Try to ensure they are not blindsided by awkward questions from upper management about their position on sustainability. At a minimum, keep key managers updated on your sustainability initiatives and associated issues.

FIGURE 5.2

Build Emotional Bank Accounts

1. Be loyal rather than duplicitous

2. Empathize with others' points of view

3. Clarify and fulfill expectations

4. Honor commitments

5. Do little things / kindnesses / courtesies

6. Apologize sincerely for "withdrawals"

Source: Based on Stephen R. Covey, *Principle-Centered Leadership*, Institute for Principle-Centered Leadership, 1990, pp. 146–47.

Bringing causes to work tends to make people uneasy, and sustainability has "cause" written all over it. If colleagues see you as a radical, tree-hugging "crud disturber" who does not respect the company's goal of being a successful business, they will marginalize you and not take you seriously. Why? Senior leaders discount dire predictions and resist making significant changes.[36] They do not want you undermining business strategies and fomenting dissent that distracts people from pressing business priorities.

In this case, your bad image is not the result of an insensitive, abrasive, interpersonal communication style; it stems from what you are promoting. To avoid this trap, you must be seen as a credible business leader before you will be accepted as a helpful sustainability leader. Do not let yourself be written off as a naive whiner, the negative "feverish, selfish little clod of ailments and grievances" described by George Bernard Shaw in Figure 5.3. Do establish your bona fides as a hard-nosed businessperson. Reassure people that you will not support sustainability strategies that might harm the bottom line. Prove that you are for the company, not against it. Play up the business benefits of sustainability initiatives and downplay the environmental and social co-benefits. Get comfortable with amping up financial reasons and damping down values-based reasons as you craft the business case for sustainability changes.[37]

Once people trust that you have the interests of the company in mind, they will relax and open up to your balanced suggestions. They will agree that the company can become more environmentally and socially responsible as a strategy for bottom-line success. You will be viewed as a valued colleague, not a problem child.

FIGURE 5.3

Shaw on the True Joy in Life

This is the true joy in life, the being used for a purpose recognized by yourself as a mighty one;...the being a force of Nature instead of a feverish selfish little clod of ailments and grievances complaining that the world will not devote itself to making you happy.

   I am of the opinion that my life belongs to the whole community and as I live it is my privilege — my *privilege* to do for it whatever I can. I want to be thoroughly used up when I die, for the harder I work the more I love. I rejoice in life for its own sake. Life is no brief candle to me; it is a sort of splendid torch which I've got a hold of for the moment and I want to make it burn as brightly as possible before handing it on to future generations.

Source: Michael and Laura Moncur, The Quotations Page website (quotations page.com/quote/23028.html).

All start, no go. All talk, no action. How would you like those monikers? You can feel as mission-driven as you want, but you need to make sure that you follow through on your rhetoric with early wins that yield credible results.

Your challenge is to marry awareness with action. Once your vision moves from theory to practice, you are more likely to get others' attention and mobilize their commitment. Frame the metrics of results from sustainability initiatives in mainstream business terms and ensure they are sophisticated enough to meet company standards for credibility.

Andrew Savitz encourages companies to find the "sustainability sweet spot" at the intersection of business interests (e.g., increased profit, increased market share, reduced costs, reduced business risk) and non-financial stakeholder interests (e.g., addressing climate change, enhancing water access, conserving natural resources, improving public health), as shown in Figure 5.4.[38] The overlap will only be sweet if it produces business results. By doing pilots, implementing prototypes, and measuring and reporting results, you prove that sustainability strategies are good for society as well as for the business. Until then, the benefits are simply theoretical.

It is also important that you not let performance in your "day job" slip as you get excited about sustainability-oriented results. Especially at the outset, sustainability objectives will not likely be part of your personal performance objectives. Excel at both your formal performance targets and your informal sustainability leadership objectives or people will think you are covering up your shortcomings with a sustainability smokescreen. Show that sustainability-oriented approaches facilitate your business performance results and do not detract from them.

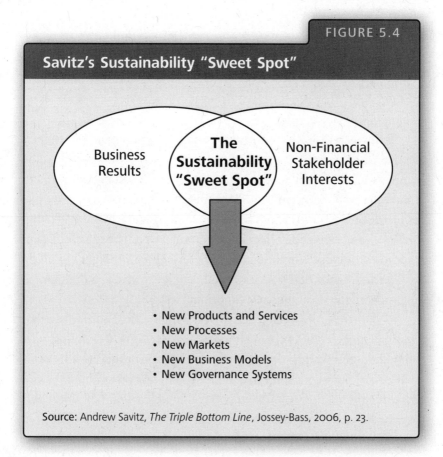

FIGURE 5.4

Savitz's Sustainability "Sweet Spot"

Business Results

The Sustainability "Sweet Spot"

Non-Financial Stakeholder Interests

- New Products and Services
- New Processes
- New Markets
- New Business Models
- New Governance Systems

Source: Andrew Savitz, *The Triple Bottom Line*, Jossey-Bass, 2006, p. 23.

Sustainability may not be stressful, but it can be a stress carrier in a few ways.

First, you will likely confront skepticism, cynicism, and resistance. People will question many things: the relevance of sustainability to the business agenda; your motives for undertaking a sustainability champion role; even the scientific underpinnings of ecological concerns like climate change. If you are not confident about your facts and leadership ability — and if you don't like confrontation — it can be stressful. Maintain your composure in the face of opposers' Three Ds (Figure 5.5). Rely on your resilience, determination, and courage to give you the stamina to deal with the frustration and emotional toll.

Second, the growing urgency to deal with the Big Four Sustainability Challenges (Figure 1.5) can keep you awake at night, wondering what your children's world — or your grandchildren's, or their children's — will be like. Such concerns can energize you to take action, but they also make it hard to know when to stop, take a break, cut yourself some slack, ask for help, and pay attention to your personal sustainability. Avoid burnout; it helps no one. Do what you can to make a difference, but ensure that you are a positive, balanced role model for others you hope to engage in your sustainability transformation effort. If they witness your exhaustion, they may have second thoughts about the personal implications of being a sustainability intrapreneur.

Third, there is a chance you will be misunderstood and sidelined. Social intrapreneurs risk losing out in the race for promotions and salary raises. One coping mechanism is to redefine success and cast off traditional notions of advancement. Intrapreneurs are motivated by a desire to drive real transformation, not climb the next step up the promotional ladder. Paradoxically, they may get both.

FIGURE 5.5

The Three Ds of Opposers

Deny
- "Asbestos is safe. Genetics cause cancer, not asbestos."
- "Climate change isn't happening. It's just a natural cycle."

Dismiss
- "Okay, asbestos can cause cancer, but not this kind of cancer and not at these doses."
- "Okay, climate change is happening, but it's not because of greenhouse gases from human activities. Besides, our company's emissions are way too small to make a difference."

Discredit
- "These people are a special interest group, not experts. And they have a hidden agenda."

6. Changing Everything at Once

Humans, like organizations, can handle only a limited amount of concurrent, unsolicited change before they choke. No intrapreneurs, no matter how skilled, can turn their companies around overnight. Beware the dangers of taking on too much too quickly.

Change is usually more exciting to the changer than to the changee. Changees may see themselves as unwilling victims, besieged by unwanted adjustments to their routines, processes, workload, and, especially, mindsets. So it is not surprising that organizations often suffer from change fatigue. When they are overwhelmed by constant changes to the status quo, they end up in the Anxiety and Stress Zone, not the Flow Zone shown in Figure 5.6.

There are several ways to avoid this roadblock en route to your vision. First, involve and engage the people affected by the sustainability changes. Implementing your own ideas is a lot less stressful than implementing someone else's. It feels better to be both the changer and the changee.

Peel the sustainability onion one layer at a time. Start with early eco-efficiency wins in sustainable operations. Then work on sustainable products and services, followed by supply chain considerations. After that base is in place, you can take on governance considerations. You may scare off executives by talking about governance changes too soon and unnecessarily.

Capitalize on the ways sustainability can synergize existing projects that may be causing the change fatigue. Show how sustainability can be a unifying force by reframing other projects as contributors to the exciting sustainability journey. Sustainability will add energy, cohesion, and meaning to a collection of seemingly disparate, debilitating changes.

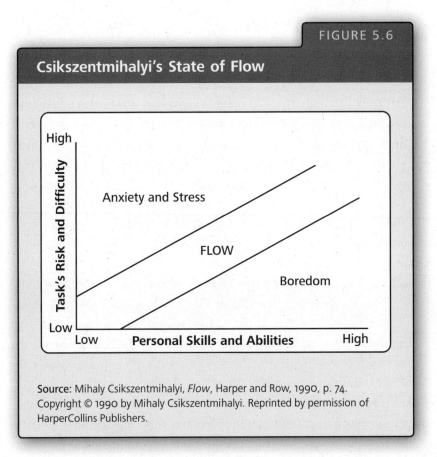

FIGURE 5.6

Csikszentmihalyi's State of Flow

Source: Mihaly Csikszentmihalyi, *Flow*, Harper and Row, 1990, p. 74.
Copyright © 1990 by Mihaly Csikszentmihalyi. Reprinted by permission of
HarperCollins Publishers.

7. Getting Off to a Bad Start

"You only get one chance to make a good first impression." That is a valid adage for job interviews, first dates, advertising, and aspiring sustainability champions.

Any of the previous six derailers can trigger a bad start. A stumble could be caused by overmanaging and underleading, by failing to delegate, or by not building a team of kindred spirits. A roadblock may spring up if you make executives unduly nervous by suggesting the company is selling the wrong products to the wrong customers using the wrong business model. That claim may be true, but leading with such accusations will result in a permanently negative first impression.

"T'ain't what you do, it's the way that you do it" is more than an Ella Fitzgerald song. The lyric alludes to how crucial "moments of truth" influence people's impressions of us, epitomized by the Scandinavian Airlines example in Figure 5.7. The tone we use, our body language and facial expressions, our eye contact or lack of it, an insensitive throwaway line meant as a joke, the way we handle distractions and interruptions or show that we are paying attention or not — all of these are elements of "moments of truth" that are continuously happening to us.

The insidious aspect of impressions, first or otherwise, is that you are usually oblivious to them. The lasting impact of bad "moments of truth" during initial encounters may be an unexpected derailer that you need to remedy. The best and easiest way to avoid this extra work is to be aware of all the "moments of truth" elements in your encounters and to consciously ensure they are positive. By being authentic and genuine, by making sincere deposits in people's emotional bank accounts, you will get off to a good start.

FIGURE 5.7

SAS's "Moments of Truth"

At SAS [Scandinavian Airlines], we used to think of ourselves as the sum total of our aircraft, our maintenance bases, our offices, and our administrative procedures. But if you ask our customers about SAS, they won't tell you about our planes or our offices or the way we influence our capital investments, they'll talk about their experiences with the people at SAS. SAS is not a collection of material assets but the quality of the contact between an individual customer and the SAS employees who serve the customer directly (or, as we refer to them, our "front line").

Last year each of our 10 million customers came in contact with approximately five SAS employees, and this contact lasted an average of 15 seconds each time. Thus SAS is "created" 50 million times a year, 15 seconds at a time. These 50 million "moments of truth" are the moments that ultimately determine whether SAS will succeed or fail as a company. They are the moments when we must prove to our customers that SAS is their best alternative.

Source: Jan Carlzon, former president of Scandinavian Airlines Systems, from his book *Moments of Truth,* pp. 2–3. Copyright © 1990 by Ballinger Publishing Company. Reprinted by permission of HarperCollins Publishers.

CHAPTER 6

Conclusion

- Think Systemically

- Push Without Being Pushy

- The Governance Question

- Lead People, Manage Processes

Sustainability champions step back and help others see the big picture. With a systems perspective, you can identify the interconnections between steps, practices, paradoxes, and derailers depicted in Figure 6.0. Such a perspective integrates the parts into a powerful, reinforcing whole.

A systems perspective helps you identify key leverage points that you need to exploit if you are to transform a company's culture. Thinking systemically lets you keep an eye on the wider marketplace and helps you distinguish major trends from random incidents. Encourage people to reflect on external patterns and trends that will alert them to emerging business threats as well as opportunities for smart sustainability strategies. Your ambition is to change the landscape of thought and practice, both internally and (eventually) externally, by re-envisioning the terms on which companies engage society.[39] That is the big societal-level picture.

Push system boundaries to see interconnections. How do sustainability initiatives in one department relate to those of other departments? How do customers' and other important stakeholders' opinions on sustainability issues affect your company? Do stakeholders expect you to be accountable for your suppliers' environmental and social impacts? Is the state of the world's ecological systems relevant to the security of your supply of materials, water, and energy?

You are pursuing the holy grail of sustainability: a better alignment between societal needs and business systems. Systems thinking lets you see the limitless possibilities to create new forms of corporate value by helping your company meet societal challenges.

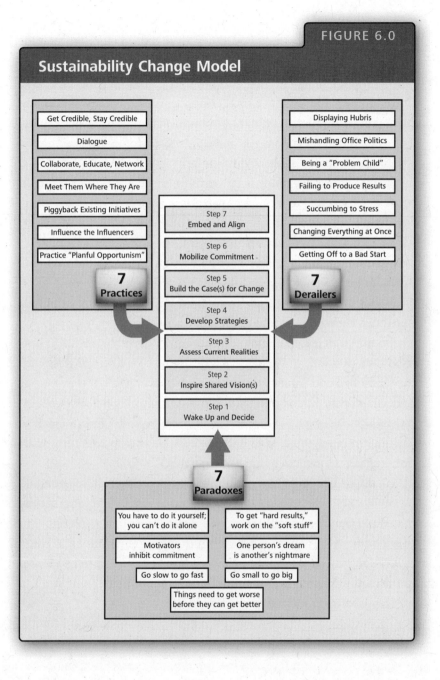

FIGURE 6.0

Sustainability Change Model

Get Credible, Stay Credible

Dialogue

Collaborate, Educate, Network

Meet Them Where They Are

Piggyback Existing Initiatives

Influence the Influencers

Practice "Planful Opportunism"

7 Practices

Displaying Hubris

Mishandling Office Politics

Being a "Problem Child"

Failing to Produce Results

Succumbing to Stress

Changing Everything at Once

Getting Off to a Bad Start

7 Derailers

Step 7
Embed and Align

Step 6
Mobilize Commitment

Step 5
Build the Case(s) for Change

Step 4
Develop Strategies

Step 3
Assess Current Realities

Step 2
Inspire Shared Vision(s)

Step 1
Wake Up and Decide

7 Paradoxes

You have to do it yourself; you can't do it alone

To get "hard results," work on the "soft stuff"

Motivators inhibit commitment

One person's dream is another's nightmare

Go slow to go fast

Go small to go big

Things need to get worse before they can get better

Driven by a sense of urgency and personal passion, sustainability champions and senior sustainability teams may be tempted to push too hard. The irony is that the harder you push, the more people will push back.

Consider Aesop's fable of the North Wind and the Sun (Figure 6.1) and its moral: Persuasion is better than force. This adage relates to all seven steps, seven practices, seven paradoxes, and seven derailers. Smart sustainability champions know when to push and when to hold back. They practice the art of leadership by gently nudging others along their personal sustainability journeys at a pace that works for each individual. Trying to go too far, too fast, will trigger defense mechanisms in an organization that is not yet ready to accept sustainability culture changes. Avoid this tripwire along the sustainability path.

Do not underestimate how much interpersonal relationships contribute to innovation. People make decisions based on conversations they have had and information they have exchanged.[40] If they do not understand your intent, or if they distrust it, they may perceive your vision as a smokescreen for hidden agendas and personal ambitions. Take the time to cover these bases and you may be able to make organizational changes more easily and more quickly.

Finally, do not underestimate the readiness of others in your organization to support your initiatives. The "blessed unrest" in global society that Paul Hawken describes so eloquently includes many colleagues in your company.[41] They want action on social and environmental issues that endanger global civilization and want their company to be a leader in the required systemic changes. They are ready to help.

So push determinedly, but push gently.

FIGURE 6.1

Aesop's Fable: The North Wind and the Sun

A dispute arose between the North Wind and the Sun, each claiming that he was stronger than the other. At last they agreed to try their powers upon a traveler to see which could soonest strip him of his cloak. The North Wind had the first try.

Gathering up all his force for the attack, he came whirling furiously down upon the man and caught up his cloak as though he would wrest it from him by one single effort: but the harder he blew, the more closely the man wrapped it round himself.

Then came the turn of the Sun. At first he beamed gently upon the traveler, who soon unclasped his cloak and walked on with it hanging loosely about his shoulders. Then he shone forth in his full strength, and the man, before he had gone many steps, was glad to throw his cloak right off and complete his journey more lightly clad.

Moral: Persuasion is better than force.

Source: 4literature website (4literature.net/Aesop/North-Wind_and_the_Sun/).

Changing a company's governance system can be the trickiest facet of a transformation to sustainability. The governance system determines how policies are institutionalized, how strategic decisions are made, how information is shared, and who has power. Top-down or hierarchical governance is a sacred cow of today's corporate model, and executives may perceive your suggestions for change as too personally threatening to consider. If you present governance system changes as a means to business-related ends, you have a fighting chance. If such changes are seen as an end in themselves, expect resistance.

Under sustainable governance, power and authority are distributed throughout the organization. Mechanisms for strategic decision making and resource allocation are more transparent. Information is freely shared with employees. Why? Because trusted employees will enthusiastically contribute their creative ideas to the transformation, improving business results. Senior leadership will become more comfortable with new approaches to governance as it sees the benefits (business success and growth) of diffusing sustainability mindsets throughout its operations.

You can avoid the blunders that impede sustainability transformation (see Figure 6.2) by revamping the governance and management system. A cohesive sense of purpose and a collective capacity to respond quickly to change replace a top-down, patriarchal system.[42]

Can a company behave sustainably without shaking up its hierarchical governance system? Yes. Can a company be an outrageously successful, regenerative enterprise without transforming its governance system? Some would say not. It depends on your views about the importance of energized, empowered employees to long-term company success.

FIGURE 6.2

Doppelt's Seven Sustainability Blunders

Blunder 1: Patriarchal/hierarchical thinking
Remedy: Empower everyone to take personal responsibility for sustainability and to commit to making it happen.

Blunder 2: "Siloed" approach to sustainability issues
Remedy: Empower everyone to use sustainability as a screen for their daily decisions/actions.

Blunder 3: No clear vision of sustainability
Remedy: Revitalize the company's goals, principles, and purpose with a positive, shared, sustainability vision.

Blunder 4: Confusion over cause and effect
Remedy: Design the root causes of emissions and discharges out of products and processes.

Blunder 5: Lack of information
Remedy: Constantly reinforce the purpose and benefits of the company becoming more sustainable.

Blunder 6: Insufficient mechanisms for learning
Remedy: Allow employees to learn by doing and reward their courageous, shared efforts.

Blunder 7: Failure to institutionalize sustainability
Remedy: Align visions, strategies, measurements, management systems, reward systems, and performance evaluation systems with sustainability principles and policies.

Source: Bob Doppelt, *Leading Change toward Sustainability,* Greenleaf Publishing, 2003, p. 88.

Leadership is about using the practices and paradoxes, and avoiding the derailers. All are people-related. Leadership is based on influence and trusting relationships. It is the capacity to translate vision into reality. Leadership credibility is earned by displaying good judgment, business acumen, and superior communication skills.

Leadership is a role, not a position. It is the art of leading people individually, in networks, inside your department, in other departments, above or below you in the organizational hierarchy, and outside your company. Anyone at any level within a company can be a legitimate sustainability leader/champion. Executive-level sustainability leaders have the luxury of short-circuiting parts of the change process, yet they can benefit from all the advice in this guidebook.

Management is about overseeing the seven-step sustainability change process. It is the science of measuring, monitoring, documenting, and getting results using proven tools. It ensures that sustainability pilots are completed on time and within budget. It requires that you have a plan for change and that you execute it while staying flexible on ways to achieve its goals.

Figure 6.3 contrasts leadership with management. Too easily, we assign value judgments to each role based on their characteristics. One is not better than the other. Depending on the situation, either style is appropriate. Effective sustainability intrapreneurs are not leaders or managers; they are leader-managers who apply sustainability leadership practices, use organizational change paradoxes, and avoid sustainability transformation derailers while managing the seven-step sustainability change process. Smart sustainability champions use a leader-manager blend to get breakthrough results. They see the sustainability vision... and go for it!

FIGURE 6.3

The Leader-Manager Blend

LEADERS AND LEADERSHIP	MANAGERS AND MANAGEMENT
Leadership is about people and relationships	Management is about processes and tasks
Leading is coaching, empowering, facilitating, serving	Managing is planning, controlling, directing
Leading is doing the right things	Managing is doing things right
Leaders lead change between paradigms	Managers maintain the status quo within paradigms
Leaders earn power based on their credibility	Managers have appointed, positional power
Leaders support innovation	Managers crave order
Leaders inspire faith in new directions	Managers demand proof
Leaders rely on trust	Managers rely on control
Leaders ask, "What/Why?"	Managers ask, "How?"
Leaders set the direction	Managers get us there

Seven Personal and Organizational Change Models

Many organizational change frameworks and leas are sprinkled throughout this guidebook, gleaned from the literature on change leadership and sustainability. In this appendix I briefly describe seven more change models that may be useful references for sustainability champions.

First, Fisher's personal transition curve depicts how individuals handle significant personal change. It applies to the first step in the seven-step change process (Wake Up and Decide) and explains what might be going through your colleagues' minds if they have trouble engaging with sustainability.

The next three models apply to both personal and organizational change. Covey's first three habits illustrate how you make the decision to lead your company on a sustainability transformation; the last four habits suggest how you might lead it effectively. Ainsworth-Land's universal S-shaped growth curve applies to all living things: plants, animals, people, teams, networks, organizations, and societies. McKenzie-Mohr's steps for community-based social-marketing show how you might change citizens' habits so that sustainable behaviors become the new norm.

The last three models focus on organizational change. Kotter's stages of organizational change echo the seven-step sustainability change process outlined in Chapter 2. Senge's five disciplines of a learning organization describe how organizations learn to stay change-ready. Rogers' model lists the attributes that accelerate an innovation's adoption by an organization — it is a wonderful way to reframe the process of spreading sustainability mindsets throughout the organizational culture.

Collectively, these change models reinforce each other and the rest of this guidebook.

Seven Personal and Organizational Change Models

CHANGE MODEL	PERSONAL CHANGE	ORGANIZATIONAL CHANGE
Fisher's Personal Transition Curve	✔	
Covey's Seven Habits of Highly Effective People	✔	✔
Ainsworth-Land's Growth Curve	✔	✔
McKenzie-Mohr's Community-Based Social Marketing	✔	✔
Kotter's Eight-Stage Organizational Change Process		✔
Senge's Five Disciplines of Learning Organizations		✔
Rogers' Five Attributes of Innovations for Fast Adoption		✔

1. Fisher's Personal Transition Curve

Skeptical people undergo personal change as they accept the relevance of sustainability to their role and the company. The personal transition curve described by John Fisher (Figure A.1) is a useful reference that may help you understand how colleagues are dealing with personal change as they adopt new, more sustainable behaviors.

According to Fisher, colleagues may start with anxiety about external threats to company success. Then they are happy that exciting change is afoot — they experience a first blush of enthusiasm about the possibility that sustainability strategies will address external threats.

As they come to understand what a truly sustainable enterprise entails, they may be overwhelmed and deny that any changes are required. If their self-perceptions, personal worldviews, belief systems, and past behaviors conflict with sustainability ideas, they may threaten not to support sustainability if it requires profound changes to those core beliefs and behaviors.

Guilt about past behaviors may be followed by depression and disillusionment because their personal beliefs and corporate core values appear to be incompatible with sustainability values. In conversations with skeptical executives, you need to acknowledge this reality and look for compatibilities with their current worldview. Meet them where they are. Through dialogue, help them progress along the curve to gradual acceptance. Then move forward.

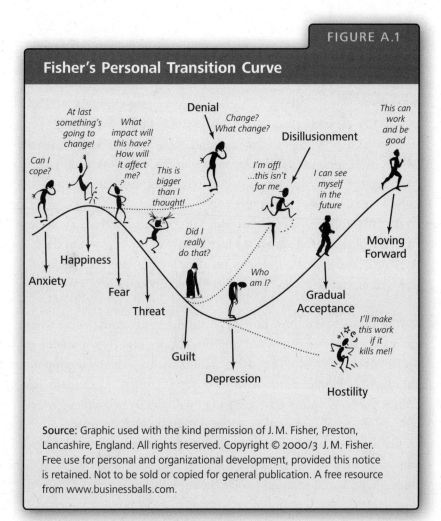

Fisher's Personal Transition Curve

At last something's going to change!

What impact will this have? How will it affect me?

Can I cope?

This is bigger than I thought!

Denial

Change? What change?

Disillusionment

I'm off! ...this isn't for me

I can see myself in the future

This can work and be good

Happiness

Anxiety

Fear

Threat

Did I really do that?

Who am I?

Gradual Acceptance

Moving Forward

I'll make this work if it kills me!!

Guilt

Depression

Hostility

2. Covey's Seven Habits of Highly Effective People

Stephen R. Covey's habits of highly effective people (Figure A.2) are universally relevant to leading personal and organizational change. The seven habits apply to personal relationships, selling, leadership, teamwork, and organizational change management. More specifically, they reinforce the leadership practices and paradoxes you will use throughout the sustainability change process.

The first three habits are embedded in the initial Wake Up and Decide step of the change process. Once sustainability champions decide to be proactive (Habit 1) and envision a sustainable enterprise (Habit 2), they put a priority on leading the sustainability transformation (Habit 3).

Habits 4, 5, and 6 show how to positively engage with people when proposing something they had not thought of doing, not intended to do, or not desired to do. The advice to think win/win (Habit 4) supports the idea of building a portfolio of visions and business cases to mobilize commitment — ensure that companies will win by becoming sustainable; otherwise, do not encourage them to adopt such strategies.

For passionate sustainability champions, Habit 5 can be the most important and the most difficult: seek first to understand, then to be understood. Using respectful and validating dialogue, seek first to understand executives' terminology, concerns, and mindsets rather than launching into a tirade about why the company should be more corporately responsible. Only then will executives consider synergizing their ideas with yours (Habit 6). Be flexible and open to minimize residual negativity that can slow progress. By sharpening the saw (Habit 7), continuing to hone and develop skills, you remain a credible, competent leader throughout the change process...and maintain your personal sustainability.

Covey's Seven Habits of Highly Effective People

Habit 1: **Be proactive**

Habit 2: **Begin with the end in mind**

Habit 3: **Put first things first**

Habit 4: **Think win / win or no deal**

Habit 5: **Seek first to understand, then to be understood**

Habit 6: **Synergize**

Habit 7: **Sharpen the saw**

Source: Stephen R. Covey, *The 7 Habits of Highly Effective People,* Simon and Schuster, 1989, p. 53.

3. Ainsworth-Land's Growth Curve

George Ainsworth-Land's transformation theory refers to evolutionary change that is inherent in all living systems, whether they are plants, fish, animals, people, teams, or companies. Ainsworth-Land's transformation theory is depicted as a series of interlocking S-curves, each with three distinct phases of growth (Figure A.3).

The Startup phase is characterized by experimentation, in which the system attempts to find a formula for survival and success. If a startup company survives the entrepreneurial stage, it institutionalizes its formula for success in the Growth phase and enjoys success until something changes in the external environment. At this point it needs to let go of the status quo and jump to a new growth curve in the Transformation phase. Failure to successfully transform results in Organizational Death.

The Transformation phase is the most relevant to sustainability change. In this phase, organizations are open to new ideas because external market forces have caused them to realize their old ideas are no longer working. Timing is critical for the introduction of innovative sustainability strategies that ensure business success. If they are suggested too early in the Growth phase, they will be rejected because the company does not need them. Things are fine; why change? On the other hand, if the strategies are proposed too late, the company may have lost resources required for the jump to a new, sustainability-enabled growth curve.

Sustainability champions may need to wait patiently for the convergence of marketplace risks and opportunities that will drive the transformation, making executives receptive to business strategies that mitigate market threats and put the company on a new growth trajectory.

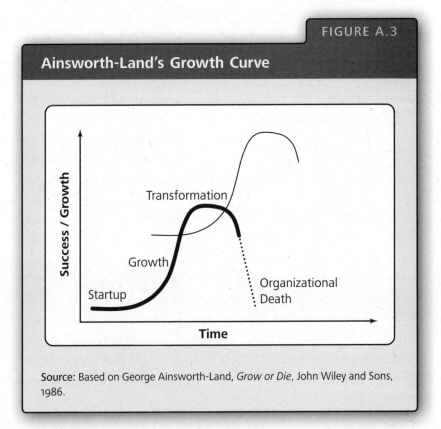

FIGURE A.3

Ainsworth-Land's Growth Curve

Source: Based on George Ainsworth-Land, *Grow or Die*, John Wiley and Sons, 1986.

4. McKenzie-Mohr's Community-Based Social Marketing

Social marketing is "the design, implementation, and control of programs seeking to increase the acceptability of a social idea, cause, or practice among a target group."[43] The social marketing steps recommended by Doug McKenzie-Mohr (Figure A.4) apply as much to embedding social and environmental practices in a target corporate culture as they do to embedding them in a community.

A sobering finding of McKenzie-Mohr's research is that information campaigns and attitude-changing initiatives have little effect on behavior. The relationship between knowledge and/or attitudes and behavior is minimal, even if the knowledge includes the financial benefits of changing behavior.[44] The benefits have to be proven.

Social marketing uses respected personal contacts to encourage a group's commitment to new behavior. This idea reinforces the importance of influencing executives through their trusted inner circles rather than by making direct contact as a stranger. It explains why building a network of respected networks is so important.

Social marketing also uses visible and timely prompts, and it tries to make new behavior as convenient as possible. This is wise advice for sustainability policy makers who are crafting incentives and penalties to encourage more sustainable behaviors.

Effective corporate sustainability champions are smart social marketers. They continuously monitor executive and company behaviors to ensure change actions are being taken and not just espoused. They create awareness, engage influencers of key executives, and use the traditional change tools and methodologies described in this guide.

McKenzie-Mohr's Community-Based Social Marketing

1. **Identify barriers and benefits**
   - Internal
   - External

2. **Use tools to change behavior**
   - Encourage written/public/group commitments
   - Establish new community norms
   - Make it convenient
   - Provide timely/vivid/positive prompts
   - Use existing personal contacts to make appeals

3. **Pilot the strategy**
   - Contain the investment cost
   - Refine it until it is effective
   - Demonstrate the program works
   - Communicate the concrete results

4. **Evaluate the strategy**
   - Measure behavior changes
   - Refine the techniques for the next time

Source: Doug McKenzie-Mohr and William Smith, *Fostering Sustainable Behavior,* New Society Publishers, 1999, pp. 15–17.

John Kotter's eight stages of major organizational change (Figure A.5) provide a useful framework for the disciplined leadership of change in companies. I drew on the strategies he recommends for leading change in large companies to produce the seven-step sustainability change process outlined in this guidebook.

During the change process, Kotter's Sense of Urgency is felt organizationally when the Build the Case(s) for Change step highlights the marketplace risks of doing nothing and the benefits from sustainability-related business opportunities. You create a Guiding Coalition when you Mobilize Commitment, building a network of kindred spirits and, ultimately, the senior-level Sustainability Team.

Four more of Kotter's stages relate to the Mobilize Commitment step:

- Communicating the Change Vision energizes all employees to contribute innovative ideas in support of sustainability goals.
- You Empower Broad-Based Action as the network of networks spreads the news and helps accelerate the company's sustainability journey.
- Pilot projects that capture eco-efficiencies Generate Short-Term Wins and help build traction.
- When you Communicate Gains and Produce More Change, momentum builds as the ripple effect spreads through the organization.

The seven-step sustainability change process reframes Kotter's advice for sustainability champions at any level in the organization, even if they do not have the position power and mandate to make it happen.

Kotter's Eight-Stage Organizational Change Process

- Establish a Sense of Urgency

- Create the Guiding Coalition

- Develop a Vision and Strategy

- Communicate the Change Vision

- Empower Broad-Based Action

- Generate Short-Term Wins

- Communicate Gains and Produce More Change

- Anchor New Approaches in the Culture

Source: John P. Kotter, *Leading Change,* Harvard Business School Press, 1996, p. 21.

6. Senge's Five Disciplines of Learning Organizations

Peter Senge's five disciplines of a learning organization (Figure A.6) are relevant if you wish to engage colleagues and executives throughout your company in corporate responsibility initiatives.

To be credible as a sustainability expert, an organizational change leader, and a business leader, you must build your Personal Mastery. Mastering sensitive communication skills helps avoid the hubris derailer.

Mental Models are synonymous with mindsets. They determine how people see the world, what they believe to be true, what they assume about how things work, and how they filter data and experiences. People are usually locked in their paradigms, discarding contrary evidence that threatens their biases. Using the practices, steps, and paradoxes outlined in this book, sustainability champions help convince skeptics to change their Mental Models.

The second step in the sustainability change process, Inspire Shared Visions, is echoed in the 3rd discipline. Sustainability champions excite others about possible new corporate futures. This excitement spirals through the organizational hierarchy, energizing others to contribute to the momentum.

Team Learning reminds us that teams empower themselves as they gain confidence while learning from their successes and failures. They learn how to make decisions and share accountability under a sustainable governance system.

Finally, Systems Thinking encourages us to look at the holistic picture of interdependencies among economic, social, and environmental aspects of a company's operations. Only when executives integrate the relationships between those three dimensions of sustainability into their mental models will they personally commit to shared visions of a sustainable enterprise.

Senge's Five Disciplines of Learning Organizations

The 1st Discipline: **Personal Mastery**

The 2nd Discipline: **Mental Models**

The 3rd Discipline: **Shared Vision**

The 4th Discipline: **Team Learning**

The 5th Discipline: **Systems Thinking**

Source: Peter M. Senge et al., *The Fifth Discipline Fieldbook,* Doubleday, 1994, p. 6. Copyright © 1994 by Peter M. Senge, Charlotte Roberts, Richard B. Ross, Bryan J. Smith, and Art Kleiner. Used by permission of Doubleday, a division of Random House, Inc.

7. Rogers' Five Attributes of Innovations for Fast Adoption

When viewed through the lens of traditional business strategies, sustainability is an innovation. It is different. Everett Rogers describes five attributes that affect the speed with which new, innovative products enter the marketplace (Figure A.7). The attributes are also relevant when you wish to disseminate a new concept, like sustainability, throughout an organization's culture.

How do you ensure a sustainability strategy contains the five attributes required for fast adoption? If executive leadership agrees to a quantified business case that acknowledges sustainability as a differentiator in the marketplace, the Relative Advantage attribute is covered. Usually corporate values resonate with a sustainability-based ethic, or sustainability initiatives can piggyback on an existing high-priority focus area, so the Compatibility characteristic is fulfilled.

The Complexity attribute may be more difficult to achieve. The good news is that sustainability is holistic and touches all aspects of company operations, but its systemic relevance is also its Achilles heel. It may seem too comprehensive to undertake. Offsetting this complexity, many aspects of sustainability lend themselves to Trialability and Observability. You can undertake small, quick-hit, pilot projects before making a company-wide commitment.

Rogers' attributes show how executives can comfortably embrace sustainability as an innovative strategy. Can sustainability be positioned so that it resonates with existing corporate values and priorities? Yes. Can it provide a quantifiable competitive advantage? Yes. Is it doable in stages? Absolutely.

Let's get on with it.

Rogers' Five Attributes of Innovations for Fast Adoption

1. **Relative Advantage**

   The innovation yields economic, status, and competitive benefits.

2. **Compatibility**

   The innovation aligns with the organization's values, beliefs, needs, and previously adopted innovations.

3. **Complexity**

   It is easy to grasp the concept.

4. **Trialability**

   It is easy to try a pilot before committing major resources.

5. **Observability**

   The benefits are evident and quickly achieved.

Source: Adapted with the permission of The Free Press, a division of Simon and Schuster Inc., from *Diffusion of Innovations*, 4th ed., by Everett M. Rogers, p. 207. Copyright © 1995 by Everett M. Rogers. Copyright © 1962, 1971, 1983 by The Free Press. All rights reserved.

Bibliography

As mentioned in the Acknowledgments, there are many authors to whom I am indebted for shaping my thinking about leadership and organizational change. Before suggesting a useful subset of their books, I'd like to mention an online resource for sustainability champions.

The International Society of Sustainability Professionals (ISSP) is a global professional association supporting sustainability practitioners. As the society says on its website (sustainabilityprofessionals.org), "We offer networking opportunities, a databank of useful resources, and professional development primarily via user-friendly web tools." In the interests of full disclosure, I am one of ISSP's founding members, but all the credit for the initiative goes to Marsha Willard (we are not related, as far as we can determine) and Darcy Hitchcock, co-founders of Axis Performance Advisors in Portland, Oregon. Through ISSP, they provide a rich set of resources and a network of kindred spirits for fellow sustainability champions.

There are four other sets of resources outlined in this bibliography.

- Ten Online News Clip Services and Blogs

- Ten Good Books on Personal Leadership

- Ten Good Books on Leading Organizational Change

- Twenty Good Books on Transforming to a Sustainable Enterprise

10 Online News Clip Services and Blogs

Sustainability intrepreneurs' credibility is enhanced if they are up to date on corporate and world sustainability news. Subscriptions to several news clip services and blogs can help.

1. **Globe-Net** is a useful news clip service. globe-net.ca/registry

2. **CSRwire** issues weekly alerts about news, events, and press releases. csrwire.com/news-alerts

3. Joel Makower's **Two Steps Forward** blog provides excellent context. makower.com/

4. **WBCSD** provides several business and sustainability news clip choices. wbcsd.org/plugins/workspace/default.asp?WSpaceId=Mjg

5. **Sustainable Business News** provides several news clip choices. sustainablelifemedia.com/newsletters

6. The **GreenBiz** newsletter features stories about the environment and business. greenbiz.com/enewsletter/

7. Tyler Hamilton's **Clean Break** blog offers clean tech news. tyler.blogware.com/

8. **World Changing** is an upbeat blog about progress on societal sustainability. worldchanging.com/

9. **Planet Ark** is Reuters' daily world environment news. planetark.com/dailynewshome.cfm

10. (Add a news clip service related to your company's industry.)

10 Good Books on Personal Leadership

This is the shortlist of books on personal leadership I relied on during my ten years in the Leadership Development department at IBM. Their guidance is timeless. They are listed alphabetically, by author surname.

1. Bennis, Warren, *On Becoming a Leader,* Addison Wesley, 1989.

2. Blanchard, Ken, Patricia Zigarmi, and Drea Zigarmi, *Leadership and the One Minute Manager,* William Morrow and Company, 1985.

3. Buckingham, Marcus, and Curt Hoffman, *First Break All the Rules,* Simon and Schuster, 1999.

4. Byham, William C., with Jeff Cox, *Zapp! The Lightning of Empowerment,* Fawcett Columbine, 1988.

5. Conner, Daryl, *Managing at the Speed of Change,* Villard Books, 1993.

6. Covey, Stephen R., *The 7 Habits of Highly Effective People,* Fireside Books, 1989.

7. Covey, Stephen R., *Principle-Centered Leadership,* Institute for Principle-Centered Leadership, 1990.

8. DePree, Max, *Leadership Is an Art,* Dell, 1989.

9. Kouzes, James M., and Barry Z. Posner, *Credibility,* Jossey-Bass, 1993.

10. Whitmore, John, *Coaching for Performance,* 3rd edition, Nicholas Brealey, 2003.

10 Good Books on Leading Organizational Change

If I had to cull my library of organizational change books down to just ten, these would make the cut. They are listed in alphabetic sequence by author surname.

1. Anderson, Linda Ackerman, and Dean Anderson, *The Change Leader's Roadmap*, Pfeiffer, 2001

2. Argryis, Chris, *Overcoming Organizational Defenses,* Allyn and Bacon, 1990.

3. Collins, James C., and Jerry I. Porras, *Built to Last,* HarperCollins, 1994.

4. Collins, Jim, *Good to Great,* HarperBusiness, 2001.

5. Cooperrider, David L., Diana Whitney, and Jacqueline M. Stavros, *The Appreciative Inquiry Handbook*, Berrett-Koehler, 2008.

6. Kotter, John P., *Leading Change,* Harvard Business School Press, 1996.

7. Kouzes, James M., and Barry Z. Posner, *The Leadership Challenge*, Jossey-Bass, 1995.

8. Rogers, Everett M., *Diffusion of Innovations,* 4th edition, John Wiley and Sons, 1998.

9. Senge, Peter M., Charlotte Roberts, Richard B. Ross, Bryan J. Smith, and Art Kleiner, *The Fifth Discipline Fieldbook,* Doubleday, 1994.

10. Senge, Peter M., Art Kleiner, Charlotte Roberts, Richard Ross, George Roth, and Bryan Smith, *The Dance of Change,* Doubleday, 1999.

20 Good Books on Transforming to a Sustainable Enterprise

Given the explosion of excellent books in this area, narrowing the list to ten was impossible. In alphabetic sequence by author surname, here are twenty.

1. Anderson, Ray C., *Mid-Course Correction*, Peregrinzilla Press, 1998.
2. AtKisson, Alan, *The ISIS Agreement*, Earthscan, 2008.
3. Blackburn, William R., *The Sustainability Handbook*, Environmental Law Institute, 2007.
4. Cleveland, Josh, ed., *Making Your Impact at Work*, Net Impact e-publication resource at netimpact.org/, 2009.
5. Doppelt, Bob, *Leading Change toward Sustainability*, Earthscan, 2003.
6. Doppelt, Bob, *The Power of Sustainable Thinking*, Earthscan, 2008.
7. Dunphy, Dexter, Andrew Griffiths, and Suzanne Benn, *Organizational Change for Corporate Sustainability*, 2nd edition, Routledge, 2003.
8. Elkington, John, *Social Intrapreneurs*, Sustainability Ltd., 2008.
9. Epstein, Marc J., *Making Sustainability Work*, Greenleaf, 2008.
10. Hart, Stuart L., *Capitalism at the Crossroads*, Wharton School Publishing, 2005.
11. Hitchcock, Darcy, and Marsha Willard, *The Step-by-Step Guide to Sustainability Planning*, Earthscan, 2008.
12. Langenwalter, Gary, *The Squeeze*, Society of Manufacturing Engineers, 2007.
13. Laszlo, Chris, *The Sustainable Company*, Island Press, 2003.
14. McKenzie-Mohr, Doug, *Fostering Sustainable Behavior*, New Society Publishers, 1999.
15. Nattrass, Brian, and Mary Altomare, *Dancing with the Tiger*, New Society Publishers, 2002.
16. Robèrt, Karl-Henrik, *The Natural Step Story*, New Society Publishers, 2002.
17. Savitz, Andrew, *The Triple Bottom Line*, Jossey-Bass, 2006.
18. Senge, Peter, Bryan Smith, Nina Kruschwitz, Joe Laur, and Sara Schley, *The Necessary Revolution*, Doubleday, 2008.
19. Sitarz, Daniel, *Greening Your Business*, EarthPress, 2008.
20. Wirtenberg, Jeana, William G. Russell, and David Lipsky, *The Sustainable Enterprise Fieldbook*, Greenleaf, 2009.

Notes

1. Gifford Pinchot, *Intrapreneuring in Action,* Berrett-Koehler, 1999.
2. Karl-Henrik Robèrt, *The Natural Step Story,* New Society Publishers, 2002, p. 246. In the late 1980s, Dr. Robèrt, with help from a broad cross-section of scientists including over 50 ecologists, chemists, physicists, and medical doctors around the world, developed a framework outlining the four conditions that are considered essential for life to be sustained on earth. The Natural Step was born.
3. Paul Hawken, Amory Lovins, and Hunter Lovins, *Natural Capitalism,* Little, Brown and Company, 1999, pp. 10–11. The authors propose four core strategies/shifts that must be in place for any enterprise to be sustainable. Each must be pursued if the enterprise's (or society's) aim is long-term harmony with natural systems. Each is interdependent, creating both constraints on and synergies with the others.
4. Bob Doppelt, *The Power of Sustainable Thinking,* Earthscan, 2008, pp. 33–34.
5. Lee Drutman, "Reinventing capitalism," a book review of *Capitalism 3.0,* by Peter Barnes, *Los Angeles Times,* January 5, 2007. Available at Lee's Word website [online], [cited September 13, 2008], ldrutman.blogspot.com/2007/01/reinventing-capitalism-los-angeles.html.
6. Peter M. Senge, Bryan Smith, Nina Kruschwitz, Joe Laur, and Sara Schley, *The Necessary Revolution,* Doubleday, 2008, p. 221. The authors list the "Big Three" core sustainability challenges of global systems: Energy and Transportation; Food and Water; Material Waste and Toxicity. To this environmentally oriented trio, I have added a fourth socially oriented challenge. I have also changed Energy and Transportation to Energy and Climate Change.
7. Ray C. Anderson, *Mid-Course Correction,* Peregrinzilla Press, 1998.
8. Peter M. Senge et al., *The Necessary Revolution,* p. 324.
9. James C. Collins and Jerry I. Porras, *Built to Last,* HarperCollins, 1994, pp. 81–114.
10. Warren Bennis, *On Becoming a Leader,* Addison Wesley, 1989, p. 192.
11. Scott Deugo, senior vice president of Design, Marketing, Continuity and Sustainable Development at Teknion, "Sustainable Development at Teknion" (PowerPoint presentation at the Schulich School of Business, York University, February 21, 2008).
12. John Elkington, *Social Intrapreneurs,* Sustainability Ltd., 2008, p. 14.
13. Ibid.

14. James M. Kouzes and Barry Z. Posner, *Credibility*, Jossey-Bass, 1993, pp. 13–18.
15. Elkington, *Social Intrapreneurs*, 2008, p. 46.
16. Scott Sonenshein, professor at Jesse H. Jones Graduate School of Management, Rice University, "Six Secrets to Selling Social Change" (PowerPoint presentation used at Net Impact's Campus Greening Initiative and Impact at Work programs, November 14, 2007).
17. Senge et al., *The Necessary Revolution*, pp. 252–55. The authors outline four types of conversation as described by Chris Argyris and C. Otto Scharmer.
18. Ibid, p. 29.
19. Sonenshein, "Six Secrets to Selling Social Change."
20. Elkington, *Social Intrapreneurs*, p. 58.
21. Michael Fullan, *The Six Secrets of Change*, Jossey-Bass, 2008, pp. 41–53.
22. Elkington, *Social Intrapreneurs*, p. 30.
23. Spreadsheets that help quantify potential business benefits from a specific company's sustainability initiatives are available at sustainabilityadvantage.com/products/index.html. One set of spreadsheets quantifies the seven areas of business benefits for large companies, as described in Bob Willard, *The Sustainability Advantage*, New Society Publishers, 2002. The other set of spreadsheets quantifies the six areas of business benefits for small and medium-sized enterprises (SMEs), as described in the appendix of Bob Willard, *The Next Sustainability Wave*, New Society Publishers, 2005. Sustainability champions are encouraged to tailor or share the spreadsheets in any way that is useful to their efforts, internally or with clients.
24. This expression was coined by Bryan Smith in his regular presentation on leading change at the Sustainable Enterprise Academy (SEA), sponsored by York University's Schulich School of Business. More information about SEA can be found at SustainableEnterpriseAcademy.org.
25. From the Quote DB website [online], [cited September 13, 2008], quotedb.com/quotes/1821.
26. Manya Arond-Thomas, "Resilient Leadership for Challenging Times," *Physician Executive*, July-August 2004, p. 18.
27. Ibid.
28. Alfie Kohn, *Punished by Rewards*, Houghton Mifflin Company, 1999.
29. Elkington, *Social Intrapreneurs*, p. 57.
30. Ibid., p. 34.
31. Bob Doppelt, *Leading Change toward Sustainability*, Greenleaf Publishing, 2003, p. 98.
32. Deugo, "Sustainable Development at Teknion."
33. Daryl Conner, *Managing at the Speed of Change*, Villard Books, 1993, pp. 92–93.

34. "Egger's Top Ten Executive Derailment Factors" [online], [cited September 13, 2008], College Planning Specialist website, 2008, collegeplanningspecialist.wordpress.com/2008/04/05/student-job-applicants-tool-1-avoid-de railing-your-career-before-it-starts/.

35. The idea of emotional bank accounts, and the suggestions in Figure 5.2, come from Stephen R. Covey, *Principle-Centered Leadership*, Institute for Principle-Centered Leadership, 1990, pp. 146–47.

36. Senge et al., *The Necessary Revolution*, p. 144.

37. Scott Sonenshein, "Crafting Social Issues at Work," *Academy of Management Journal* 49, no. 6 (2006), p. 1168.

38. Andrew Savitz, *The Triple Bottom Line*, Jossey-Bass, 2006, p. 23.

39. Elkington, *Social Intrapreneurs*, p. 55.

40. Ibid., p. 57.

41. Paul Hawken, *Blessed Unrest*, Viking, 2007, p. 12.

42. Doppelt, *Leading Change toward Sustainability*, pp. 17–18.

43. Gary Armstrong and Philip Kotler, "Glossary" in *Marketing*, 5th edition [online], [Cited September 13, 2008], Prentice Hall website, 2000, prenhall .com/divisions/bp/app/armstrong/cw/glossary.html.

44. Doug McKenzie-Mohr and William Smith, *Fostering Sustainable Behavior*, New Society Publishers, 1999, pp. 10–12.

Index

Page references in the form 122n6 direct the reader to endnotes. This one refers to note 6 on page 122.

About the Author

BOB WILLARD is a leading expert on the business value of corporate sustainability strategies. He has given hundreds of keynote presentations to corporations, governments, academics, and NGOs. Bob applies business and leadership development experience from his 34-year career at IBM Canada to engage the business community in proactively avoiding risks and capturing opportunities associated with environmental and social issues.

He is the author of *The Sustainability Advantage*, which quantifies potential bottom-line benefits from using sustainability strategies, and *The Next Sustainability Wave*, which shows how to convince senior executives to commit to sustainability strategies. His DVD presentation *The Business Case for Sustainability* is used in webinars and videoconferences and helps reduce his carbon footprint from global speaking trips.

Bob is on the faculties of the Sustainable Enterprise Academy and the Sustainability and Education Academy; is on the advisory boards of the Natural Step Canada, Durham Sustain Ability, Learning for a Sustainable Future, Transition Plus, and eQuilibrium; and is a member of the Education Alliance for a Sustainable Ontario, the International Society of Sustainability Professionals, and the Canadian Association of Professional Speakers.

He has a BSc from McGill University (1964) and an MEd (2000) and PhD (2005) from the University of Toronto. A resident of Ontario, he is the proud owner of two hybrid cars: a Honda Accord Hybrid and a Honda Civic Hybrid. More information about Bob, as well as his spreadsheet, slide, and DVD resources for sustainability champions, can be found at sustainabilityadvantage.com.

If you have enjoyed *The Sustainability Champion's Guidebook*,
you might also enjoy other

Books to Build a New Society

Our books provide positive solutions for people who want
to make a difference. We specialize in:

Sustainable Living ◆ Ecological Design and Planning

Natural Building & Appropriate Technology ◆ New Forestry

Environment and Justice ◆ Conscientious Commerce

Progressive Leadership ◆ Resistance and Community ◆ Nonviolence

Educational and Parenting Resources

For a full list of NSP's titles, please call 1-800-567-6772 or check out our web site at:

www.newsociety.com

NEW SOCIETY PUBLISHERS